watchOS 2 App Development Essentials

watchOS 2 App Development Essentials – First Edition

Rev 1.0

 eBookFrenzy

Table of Contents

1. Start Here

Announced in September 2014, the Apple Watch family of devices is Apple's first foray into the market of wearable technology. The introduction of this new device category was accompanied by the release of the WatchKit framework designed specifically to allow developers to build Apple Watch app extensions to accompany iPhone-based iOS apps. In June of 2015, Apple announced the introduction of watchOS 2, the second version of the operating system that runs on the Apple Watch. This new release of watchOS introduced a number of improvements to the performance of the Apple Watch and provided a wider range of options for developers creating WatchKit apps.

WatchOS 2 App Development Essentials is intended for readers with some existing experience of iOS development using Xcode and the Swift programming language. Beginning with the basics, this book provides an introduction to WatchKit apps and the watchOS 2 app development architecture before covering topics such as tables, navigation, user input handling, working with images, maps and menus.

More advanced topics are also covered throughout the book, including communication and data sharing between a WatchKit app and the parent iOS app, working with custom fonts, user interface animation, clock face complications and the design and implementation of custom notifications.

As with all the books in the "Development Essentials" series, watchOS 2 App Development Essentials takes a modular approach to the subject of app development for the Apple Watch, with each chapter covering a self-contained topic area consisting of detailed explanations, examples and step-by-step tutorials. This makes the book both an easy to follow learning aid and an excellent reference resource.

1.1 Source Code Download

The source code and Xcode project files for the examples contained in this book are available for download at:

http://www.ebookfrenzy.com/print/watchos2/

1.2 Download the eBook

Thank you for purchasing the print edition of this book. If you would like to download the eBook version of this book, please email proof of purchase to *feedback@ebookfrenzy.com* and we will provide you with a download link for the book in PDF, ePub and MOBI formats.

1.3 **Feedback**

We want you to be satisfied with your purchase of this book. If you find any errors in the book, or have any comments, questions or concerns please contact us at *feedback@ebookfrenzy.com*.

1.4 **Errata**

Whilst we make every effort to ensure the accuracy of the content of this book, it is inevitable that a book covering a subject area of this size and complexity may include some errors and oversights. Any known issues with the book will be outlined together with solutions at the following URL:

http://www.ebookfrenzy.com/errata/watchos2.html

In the event that you find an error not listed in the errata, please let us know by emailing our technical support team at *feedback@ebookfrenzy.com*.

2. watchOS 2 Apps – An Overview

Before embarking on the creation of a watchOS 2 app it is important to gain a basic understanding of what an Apple Watch app consists of and, more importantly, how it fits into the existing iOS application ecosystem. Within this chapter, a high level overview of watchOS 2 apps will be provided, together with an outline of how these apps are structured and delivered to the customer.

2.1 What is a watchOS App?

watchOS is the name given to the operating system that runs on the Apple Watch device. Prior to the introduction of the Apple Watch family of devices, it was only possible to develop mobile applications for iPhone, iPad and iPod Touch devices running the iOS operating system. With the introduction of the Apple Watch, however, it is now possible for iOS developers to also create apps that run on watchOS.

In simplistic terms, watchOS apps are launched on an Apple Watch device either as the result of an action by the user or in response to some form of local or remote notification. Once launched, the watchOS app presents a user interface on the watch screen displaying information and controls with which the user can interact to perform tasks.

2.2 WatchKit App or watchOS App?

iOS apps are developed using a variety of software development kit frameworks. Although a number of frameworks are also available for developing watchOS apps, the primary framework used on watchOS is the WatchKit framework.

So far in this chapter we have referred to apps running on an Apple Watch device as watchOS apps. In actual fact, these apps are more correctly referred to as *WatchKit apps*. That being said, there seems to be little consistency in the terms used to refer to an app that runs on an Apple Watch. When reading Apple's marketing and technical documentation it is not uncommon to find Apple Watch apps referred to as watch apps, WatchKit apps or watchOS apps. For the avoidance of confusion, apps designed to run on an Apple Watch will be referred to as WatchKit apps throughout the remainder of this book.

2.3 **WatchKit Apps and iOS Apps**

It is important to understand that WatchKit apps are not standalone entities. A WatchKit app can only be created as an *extension* to an existing iOS app. It is not, therefore, possible to create a WatchKit app that is not bundled as part of a new or existing iOS application.

Consider, for example, an iPhone iOS application designed to provide the user with detailed weather information. Prior to the introduction of the Apple Watch, the only way for the user to access the information provided by the app would have been to pick up the iPhone, unlock the device, launch the iOS app and view the information on the iPhone display. Now that information can be made available via the user's Apple Watch device.

In order to make the information provided by the iOS app available via the user's Apple Watch, the developer of the weather app would add a WatchKit app extension to the iOS app, design a suitable user interface to display the information on the watch display and implement the logic to display the appropriate weather information and respond to any user interaction. Instead of having to launch the iOS app from the iPhone device to check the weather, the user can now launch the WatchKit app from the Apple Watch and view and interact with the information.

Clearly, the display size of an Apple Watch is considerably smaller than that of even the smallest of iPhone models. As such, a WatchKit app will typically display only a subset of the content available on the larger iPhone screen. For more detailed information, the user would still need to make use of the iOS application.

2.4 **The watchOS SDK Frameworks**

Running directly on the hardware of the Apple Watch is the watchOS 2 operating system. Included with the operating system is a set of frameworks that combine to make up the watchOS SDK. WatchKit apps are developed by making use of the various frameworks contained within the watchOS SDK. This can best be presented visually as outlined in the diagram shown in Figure 2-1:

Figure 2-1

The key layer for the app developer is the watchOS SDK which contains a number of different frameworks. Figure 2-2 illustrates the frameworks contained within the watchOS 2 SDK that are available for use when developing apps for watchOS:

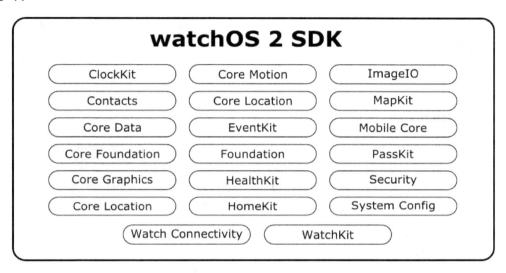

Figure 2-2

With the exception of the WatchKit and Watch Connectivity frameworks, many of these frameworks will be familiar to iOS developers, though it is important to be aware that not all of the features of a framework that are available on iOS are supported on watchOS.

2.5 The Key Components of a WatchKit App

A WatchKit app is comprised of the *Watchkit app* and a *WatchKit extension*.

Extensions are a feature introduced as part of the iOS 8 SDK release and were originally intended solely to allow certain capabilities of an application to be made available for use within other applications running on the same device. The developer of a photo editing application might, for example, have devised some unique image filtering capabilities and decide that those features would be particularly useful to users of the iOS Photos app. To achieve this, the developer would implement these features in a Photo Editing extension which would then appear as an option to users when editing an image within the Photos app. Other extension types are also available for performing document storage, creating custom keyboards and embedding information from an application into the iOS notification panel.

With the introduction of the Apple Watch and watchOS, however, the concept of extensions has now been extended to make the functionality of an iOS app available in the form of a WatchKit app.

Extensions are separate executable binaries that run independently of the corresponding iOS application. Although extensions take the form of an individual binary, they must be supplied and installed as part of an iOS application bundle. The iOS application with which an extension is bundled is referred to as the *containing app* or *parent app*. The containing app must provide useful functionality and must not be an empty application provided solely for the purpose of delivering an extension to the user.

When an iOS application containing a WatchKit app has been installed on an iPhone device, both the WatchKit app and the corresponding WatchKit extension are subsequently transferred and installed onto the paired Apple Watch device. When the user launches a WatchKit app on a watch device, the WatchKit framework will launch the corresponding WatchKit extension before beginning the app initialization process.

2.6 **Basic WatchKit App Structure**

As previously outlined, the implementation of a WatchKit app is divided between the WatchKit app and WatchKit extension, both of which reside and execute on the Apple Watch device. This raises the question of how the responsibilities of providing the functionality of the WatchKit app are divided between these components. These responsibilities may be summarized as follows:

WatchKit app – Consists of the storyboard file containing the user interface and corresponding resources (such as image and configuration files).

WatchKit Extension – Contains all of the code required to provide the functionality of the WatchKit app and responding to user interaction. The extension may also contain resources such as images and media files.

2.7 **WatchKit App Entry Points**

There are number of different ways in which the user may enter a WatchKit app, each of which will be detailed in later chapters and can be summarized as follows:

- **Home Screen** – Once installed, the WatchKit app will be represented by an icon on the home screen of the Apple Watch display. When this icon is selected by the user the app will load and display the main user interface scene.
- **Glance** – When developing a WatchKit app, the option is available to add a *Glance* interface to the app. This is a single, non-scrollable, read-only scene that can be used to display a quick-look summary of the information normally presented by the full version of the app. Glances are accessed when the user performs an upward swiping motion on the watch display and, when tapped by the user, launch the corresponding WatchKit app.
- **Notifications** – When a notification for a WatchKit app appears on the Apple Watch device, the app will be launched when the notification is tapped.

2.8 **Summary**

A WatchKit app is an application designed to run on the Apple Watch family of devices. A WatchKit app cannot be a standalone application and must instead be created as an extension of an existing iOS application. The

WatchKit app is installed on the Apple Watch device and consists of a storyboard file containing the user interface of the app together with a set of resource files. The WatchKit extension is also installed on the Apple Watch device and contains all of the code logic required to implement the behavior of the WatchKit app.

3. Building an Example WatchKit App

Having outlined the basic architecture for a WatchKit app in the previous chapter, it is now time to start putting some of this knowledge to practical use through the creation of a simple example app.

The project created in this chapter will work through the creation of a basic WatchKit app that does nothing more than display a message and an image on an Apple Watch display.

3.1 Creating the WatchKit App Project

Start Xcode and, on the Welcome screen, select the *Create a new Xcode project* option. On the template screen choose the *Application* option located under *watchOS* in the left hand panel and select *iOS App with WatchKit App*. Click *Next,* set the product name to *WatchKitSample,* enter your organization name and identifier and make sure that the *Devices* menu is set to *Universal* so that the user interface will be suitable for deployment on all iPhone and iPad screen sizes. Before clicking *Next*, change the *Language* menu to *Swift* and turn off the *Include Notification Scene* option. On the final screen, choose a file system location in which to store the project files and click on the *Create* button to proceed to the main Xcode project window.

A review of the project files within the Project Navigator panel will reveal that, in addition to the iOS app target, new folders have been added for the WatchKit Extension and the WatchKit App (Figure 3-1) each of which contains the files that will need to be modified to implement the appearance and behavior of the WatchKit app:

Figure 3-1

3.2 **Designing the iOS App User Interface**

The next step in the project is to design the user interface for the iOS app. This layout is contained within the *Main.storyboard* file and is listed in the Project Navigator panel on the left hand side of the main Xcode window. Locate and click on this file to load it into the Interface Builder environment. Once loaded, locate the Label view object in the Object Library panel and drag and drop it onto the storyboard scene. Double-click on the label and change the text so that it reads "Welcome to WatchKit" before positioning it so that it is centered in the layout canvas as illustrated in Figure 3-2:

Figure 3-2

Select the new label in the layout canvas and display the *Resolve Auto Layout Issues* menu by clicking on the button in the lower right hand corner of the Interface Builder panel as indicated in Figure 3-3:

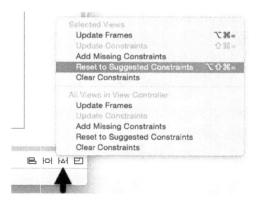

Figure 3-3

From the resulting menu, select the *Reset to Suggested Constraints* option. This will set up recommended layout constraints so that the label remains centered both horizontally and vertically within the screen regardless of whether the application is running on an iPhone or iPad display.

The user interface for the iOS application is now complete. Verify this by running the application on an iPhone device or iOS Simulator session before continuing.

3.3 Designing the WatchKit App Storyboard

The next step in the project is to design the user interface for the WatchKit app. This is contained within the *Interface.storyboard* file located under the *WatchKitSample WatchKit App* folder within the Project Navigator. Locate and select this file to load it into the Interface Builder tool where the scene will appear as illustrated in Figure 3-4:

Figure 3-4

Designing the user interface for a WatchKit app involves dragging objects from the Object Library panel onto the layout canvas. When user interface objects are added to the layout canvas they are stacked vertically. These elements are then positioned at runtime by WatchKit based on the available display space combined with any sizing and positioning attributes declared during the storyboard design phase.

For the purposes of this example, the user interface will be required to display an image and a label. Locate the Image object in the Object Library panel and drag and drop it onto the scene layout. Repeat this step to position a Label object immediately beneath the Image object. Double click on the newly added Label object and change the text so that it reads "Hello WatchKit" such that the layout matches that of Figure 3-5:

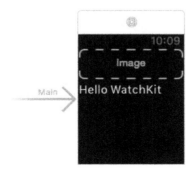

Figure 3-5

Before testing the app, some additional attributes need to be set on the objects in the user interface. The first step is to configure the Image object to display an image. Before this can be configured, however, the image file needs to be added to the project. The image file is named *watch_image@2x.png* and can be found in the *sample_images* folder of the sample code archive which can be downloaded from the following URL:

http://www.ebookfrenzy.com/print/watchos2/index.php

Within the Project Navigator panel, select the *Assets.xcassets* entry listed under *WatchKitSample WatchKit App* so that the asset catalog loads into the main panel. Locate the *watch_image@2x.png* image file in a Finder window and drag and drop it onto the left hand panel in the asset catalog as illustrated in Figure 3-6:

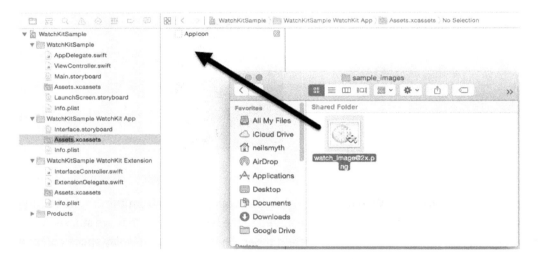

Figure 3-6

With the image file added to the project, the Image object needs to be configured to display the image when the app runs. Select the Image object in the storyboard scene and display the Attributes Inspector in the utilities panel (*View -> Utilities -> Show Attributes Inspector*). Within the inspector panel, use the drop down menu for the Image attribute to select the *watch_image* option:

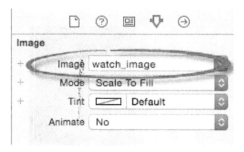

Figure 3-7

Finally, select the Label object in the scene and use the Attribute Inspector panel to change the *Alignment* attribute so that the text is centered within the label. Having set this attribute, a review of the scene will show that the text is still positioned on the left of the layout. The reason for this is that the text has been centered within the label but the Label object itself is still positioned on the left side of the display. To correct this, locate the *Alignment* section in the Attributes Inspector panel and change the *Horizontal* attribute from *Left* to *Center*. Figure 3-8 shows the Attributes Inspector panel with these attributes set:

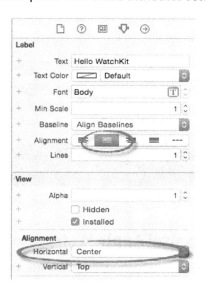

Figure 3-8

3.4 **Running the WatchKit App**

All that remains is to run the WatchKit app and make sure that it appears as expected. For the purposes of this example this will be performed using the simulator environment. In order to test the WatchKit app, the run target may need to be changed in the Xcode toolbar. Select the current scheme in the toolbar and use the drop down menu (Figure 3-9) to select the *WatchKitSample WatchKit App -> iPhone 6 + Apple Watch – 38mm* option:

Figure 3-9

With the WatchKit app selected, click on the run button. Once the simulator has loaded, two windows should appear, one representing the iPhone 6 device and the other the Apple Watch device. After a short delay, the WatchKit app should appear on the watch simulator display as illustrated in Figure 3-10:

Figure 3-10

3.5 Running the App on a Physical Apple Watch Device

In order to test the app on a physical Apple Watch device, connect an iPhone with which an Apple Watch is paired to the development system and select it as the target device within the Xcode toolbar panel (Figure 3-11).

Figure 3-11

With *WatchKitSample WatchKit App* still selected as the run target, click on the run button and wait for the app icon to appear on the Apple Watch home screen and for the app to launch.

3.6 Setting the Scene Title and Key Color

The area at the top of the Apple Watch display containing the current time is the *status bar* and the area to the left of the time is available to display a title string. To set this property, click on the scene within the storyboard so that it highlights in blue, display the Attributes Inspector panel and enter a title for the scene into the *Title* field:

Figure 3-12

The foreground color of all of the scene titles in a WatchKit app may be configured by setting the *global tint* attribute for the storyboard file. To set this property, select the *Interface.storyboard* file in the Project Navigator panel and display the File Inspector panel (*View -> Utilities -> Show File Inspector*). Within the File Inspector panel change the color setting for the *Global Tint* attribute (Figure 3-13) to a different color.

Figure 3-13

Next time the app runs, all of the titles in the scenes that make up the storyboard will be rendered using the selected foreground color.

The global tint color is also adopted by the app name when it is displayed in the short look notification panel, a topic area that will be covered in detail in the chapter entitled *An Overview of Notifications in WatchKit*.

3.7 **Adding App Icons to the Project**

Every WatchKit app must have associated with it an icon. This icon represents the app on the Apple Watch Home screen and identifies the app in notifications and within the iPhone-based Apple Watch app. A variety of icon sizes may need to be created depending on where the icon is displayed and the size of Apple Watch on which the app is running. The various icon size requirements are as outlined in Table 3-1:

Icon	38mm Watch	42mm Watch
Home Screen	80 x 80 pixels	80 x 80 pixels
Long Look Notification	80 x 80 pixels	88 x 88 pixels
Short Look Notification	172 x 172 pixels	196 x 196 pixels
Notification Center	48 x 48 pixels	55 x 55 pixels

Table 3-1

In addition to the icons in Table 3-1, icons are also required for the Apple Watch app on the paired iPhone device. Two versions of the icon are required for this purpose so that the icon can be represented on both iPhone (@2x) and iPhone Plus (@3x) size models:

Icon	iPhone @2x	iPhone Plus @3x
Apple Watch App	58 x 58 pixels	87 x 87 pixels

Table 3-2

Since the app created in this chapter does not make use of notifications, only Home Screen and Apple Watch app icons need to be added to the project. The topic of notification icons will be addressed in greater detail in the chapter entitled *A WatchKit Notification Tutorial*.

The home screen icon needs to be circular and 80x80 pixels in size with a 24-bit color depth. The image must be in PNG format with a file name ending with "@2x", for example *homeicon@2x.png*.

Icons are stored in the asset catalog of the WatchKit app target. Access the image set in the asset catalog by selecting the *Assets.xcassets* file listed under the *WatchKitSample WatchKit App* folder in the project navigator panel. Within the asset catalog panel (Figure 3-14), select the *AppIcon* image set:

Figure 3-14

To add icons, locate them in a Finder window and drag and drop them onto the corresponding location within the image set. For the purposes of this example, app icons can be found in the *app_icons* folder of the sample code download.

Once the icons have been located, drag and drop the icon file named *HomeIcon@2x.png* onto the *Apple Watch Home Screen (All)* image location within the image asset catalog as shown in Figure 3-15:

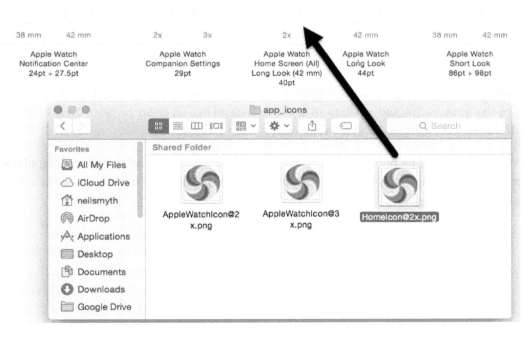

Figure 3-15

The two Apple Watch app icons are named *AppleWatchIcon@2x.png* and *AppleWatchIcon@3x.png* and should be placed in the *Apple Watch Companion Settings* 2x and 3x image locations respectively. Once these icons have been added the three icon categories in the AppIcon image set should resemble Figure 3-16:

2x   3x   2x

Apple Watch   Apple Watch
Companion Settings   Home Screen (All)
29pt   Long Look (42 mm)
                         40pt

Figure 3-16

When the sample WatchKit app is now compiled and run on either a Watch simulator or a physical Apple Watch device the app will be represented on the device Home Screen by the provided icon (the home screen can be displayed on the Simulator by selecting the *Hardware -> Home* menu option).

3.8 Summary

This chapter has worked through the steps involved in creating a simple WatchKit app and running it within the simulator environment. A WatchKit app is added as a target to an existing iOS app project. When a WatchKit target is added, Xcode creates an initial storyboard for the WatchKit app user interface and the basic code for the WatchKit Extension template. The user interface for the WatchKit app is designed in the storyboard file by selecting and positioning UI objects in the Interface Builder environment and setting attributes where necessary to configure the appearance and position of the visual elements. In order to test run a WatchKit app, the appropriate run target must first be selected from the Xcode toolbar.

Before a WatchKit app can be published, app icons must be added to the image asset catalog of the WatchKit App target. These icons must meet strict requirements in terms of size and format, details of which have also been covered in this chapter.

4. An Overview of the WatchKit App Architecture

The previous chapters have explained that a WatchKit app consists of two main components, the WatchKit app itself and the WatchKit extension.

It has also been established that the WatchKit app is primarily responsible for displaying the user interface while the programming logic of the app resides within the WatchKit extension.

It is less clear at this point, however, how the user interface elements in the app are connected to the code in the extension. In other words, how the project is structured such that tapping on a button in a scene causes a specific method in the extension to be called. Similarly, we need to understand how the code within the extension can manipulate the properties of a visual element in a storyboard scene, for example changing the text displayed on a Label interface object. These topics will be covered in this chapter and then put into practice in the next chapter entitled *An Example Interactive WatchKit App*.

This chapter will also introduce the extension delegate class and provide an overview of the lifecycle of a WatchKit app and outline the ways in which this can be used to perform certain initialization tasks when a WatchKit app is launched.

4.1 Basic WatchKit App Architecture

As discussed in previous chapters, the WatchKit app itself consists only of the storyboard file and a set of resource files. The storyboard contains one or more scenes, each of which represents a different screen within the app and may, optionally, provide mechanisms for the user to transition from one scene to another. Clearly this does not provide any functionality beyond presenting user interfaces to the user. The responsibility of providing the behavior behind a user interface scene so that the app actually does something useful belongs to the *interface controller*.

4.2 WatchKit Interface Controllers

Each scene within a storyboard must have associated with it an interface controller instance. Interface controllers are subclassed from the WatchKit framework WKInterfaceController class and contain the code that allows the WatchKit app to perform tasks beyond simply presenting a user interface to the user. This provides a separation between the user interfaces (the storyboard) and the logic code (the interface controllers). In fact, interface controllers are similar to view controllers in iOS applications.

The interface controllers for a WatchKit app reside within the WatchKit extension associated with the app and are installed and executed on the Apple Watch. It is the responsibility of the interface controller to respond to user interactions in the corresponding user interface scene and to make changes to the visual elements that make up the user interface. When a user taps a button in a WatchKit scene, for example, a method in the interface controller will be called by the WatchKit framework in order to perform some form of action. In the event that a change needs to be made to a user interface element, for example to change the text displayed on a label, the interface controller will make the necessary changes and the WatchKit framework will transmit those changes to the WatchKit app where the update will be performed.

This sounds good in theory but does not explain how the connections between the elements in the user interface and the interface controller are established. This requires an understanding of the concepts of *outlets* and *action methods*.

4.3 **WatchKit Action Methods**

Creation of a WatchKit app typically involves designing the user interface scenes using the Interface Builder tool and writing the code that provides the logic for the app in the source code files of the interface controller classes. In this section we will begin to look at how the user interface scene elements and the interface controller code interact with each other.

When a user interacts with objects in a scene of a WatchKit app, for example touching a button control, an *event* is triggered. In order for that event to achieve anything, it needs to trigger a method call on the interface controller class. Use of a technique known as *target-action* provides a way to specify what happens when such events are triggered. In other words, this is how you connect the objects in the user interface you have designed in the Interface Builder tool to the back end Swift code you have implemented in the corresponding interface controller class. Specifically, this allows you to define which method of the interface controller gets called when a user interacts in a certain way with a user interface object.

The process of wiring up a user interface object to call a specific method on an interface controller is achieved using something called an *Action*. Similarly, the target method is referred to as an *action method*. Action methods are declared within the interface controller class using the IBAction keyword, for example:

```
@IBAction func buttonPress() {
    print("Button Pressed")
    // Perform tasks in response to a button press
}
```

4.4 **WatchKit Outlets**

The opposite of an *Action* is an *Outlet*. As previously described, an Action allows a method in an interface controller instance to be called in response to a user interaction with a user interface element. An Outlet, on the other hand, allows an interface controller to make changes to the properties of a user interface element. An interface controller might, for example, need to set the text on a Label object. In order to do so, an Outlet must first have been defined using the *IBOutlet* keyword. In programming terms, an *IBOutlet* is simply an instance variable that references the user interface object to which access is required. The following line demonstrates an outlet declaration for a label:

```
@IBOutlet weak var myLabel: WKInterfaceLabel!
```

Once outlets and actions have been implemented and connected, all of the communication required to make these connections work is handled transparently by WatchKit. Figure 4-1 provides a visual representation of actions and outlets:

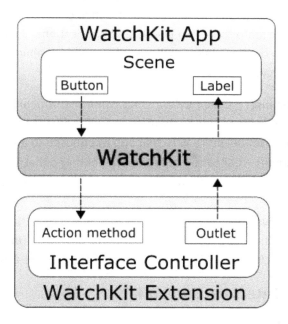

Figure 4-1

Outlets and actions can be created visually with just a few mouse clicks from within Xcode using the Interface Builder tool in conjunction with the Assistant Editor panel, a topic which will be covered in detail in the chapter entitled *An Example Interactive WatchKit App*.

4.5 **WatchKit App State Transitions**

At any given time, a WatchKit app will be in one of the following three possible states:

- **Not running** – Either the WatchKit app has yet to be launched or it has been terminated by watchOS.
- **Inactive** – The WatchKit app is running but is not receiving any events from WatchKit. An app usually enters this state briefly during the launch process, or when the app is transitioning out of active state because the user is no longer interacting with the app.
- **Active** – The WatchKit app is running, is most likely the currently visible app on the Apple Watch and is receiving events.

As a WatchKit app transitions from one state to another, the app is notified of the state change via calls to the methods in the extension delegate object.

4.6 **The WatchKit Extension Delegate**

In addition to an interface controller instance for each scene in the WatchKit app, the WatchKit extension also includes a single *extension delegate* object. This class is added to the WatchKit extension automatically by Xcode when a WatchKit app target is created and conforms to the WKExtensionDelegate protocol which defines which methods this class must implement. These methods are then called by the WatchKit framework to notify the WatchKit app about lifecycle state transition events and notifications. By adding code to these methods, the WatchKit app can respond to the notifications where necessary. At a minimum the extension delegate class will implement the following lifecycle methods:

- **applicationDidFinishLaunching()** – Called by WatchKit when the WatchKit app launch process is close to completion and the WatchKit extension is about to run. This is a useful location in which to perform initialization tasks that relate to the entire WatchKit app as opposed to an individual interface controller.
- **applicationDidBecomeActive()** – Called to notify the WatchKit app that it is now active and visible to the user. This method may be used to resume any tasks that were paused when the app previously transitioned to the inactive state.
- **applicationDidBecomeInactive()** – Called when the WatchKit app transitions from active to inactive state. This opportunity should be taken to pause any non-essential activities. Once in the inactive state, the app will either transition to the active or not running state depending on the actions of the user.

4.7 **The Lifecycle of an Interface Controller**

The lifecycle of a WatchKit app and the corresponding WatchKit extension is actually very simple. When a WatchKit app is launched on the device, a scene will be loaded from within the storyboard file. When the scene has loaded, the WatchKit framework will request that the extension corresponding to the app be launched. The extension is then instructed to create the interface controller associated with the scene that was loaded.

As long as the user is interacting with the WatchKit app the extension will continue to run. When the system detects that the user is no longer interacting with the watch, or the user exits the app, the interface controller is deactivated and the extension suspended.

At various points during this interface controller initialization and de-initialization cycle, calls will be made to specific lifecycle methods declared within the interface controller class where code can be added to perform initialization and clean up tasks. These methods are as follows:

- **init()** - The first method called on the interface controller when the scene is to be displayed. This method can be used to perform initialization tasks in preparation for the scene being displayed to the user. It is also possible to make changes to user interface objects via outlets from within this method.
- **awakeWithContext()** - This method is called after the call to the init() method and may optionally be passed additional context data. This is typically used when navigating from one scene to another in a multi-scene app and allows data to be passed from the interface controller of the currently displayed scene to the interface controller of the destination scene. Access to user interface objects is available from within this method.
- **willActivate()** – Called immediately before the scene is presented to the user on the Apple Watch device. This is the recommended method for making final minor changes to the elements in the user interface. Access to user interface objects is available from within this method.
- **didAppear()** – This method is called immediately after the scene associated with the interface controller becomes visible to the user on the Apple Watch screen. This is the recommended lifecycle method in which to initiate any animation sequences.
- **willDisappear()** – Called immediately before the scene associated with the interface controller is removed from view on the Apple Watch screen. This method should be used to stop any animation that is currently running.
- **didDeactivate()** – The last method called when the user exits the current scene or the system detects that, although the app is still running, the user is no longer interacting with the Apple Watch device. This method should be used to perform any cleanup tasks necessary to ensure a smooth return to the scene at a later time. Access to user interface objects is not available from within this method. Calls to this method may be triggered for testing purposes from within the WatchKit simulator environment by locking the simulator via the *Hardware -> Lock* menu option.

The diagram in Figure 4-2 illustrates the WatchKit app lifecycle as it corresponds to the WatchKit extension and interface controller:

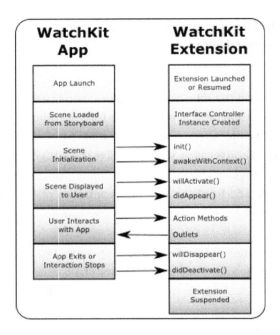

Figure 4-2

It should be noted that, with the exception of the app launch and extension suspension phases in the above diagram, the same lifecycle sequence is performed each time a scene is loaded within a running WatchKit app.

4.8 WatchKit Extension Guidelines

A key point to note from the lifecycle description is that the WatchKit extension is suspended when the user either exits or stops interacting with the WatchKit app. It is important, therefore, to avoid performing any long term tasks within the extension. Any tasks that need to continue executing after the extension has been suspended should be passed to the containing iOS app to be handled. Details of how this can be achieved are outlined in the *An Introduction to Watch Connectivity in watchOS 2* chapter of this book.

4.9 Summary

Each scene within a WatchKit app has associated with it an interface controller within the WatchKit extension. The interface controller contains the code that provides the underlying logic and behavior of the WatchKit app.

The interactions between the current scene of a WatchKit app running on an Apple Watch and the corresponding interface controller within the WatchKit extension are implemented using actions and outlets. Actions define the methods that get called in response to specific actions performed by the user within the scene. Outlets, on the other hand, provide a mechanism for the interface controller code to access and modify the properties of user interface objects.

A WatchKit app will transition through different lifecycle states consisting of not running, inactive and active. The app is notified of each transition change via a call to methods within the extension delegate.

When a WatchKit app is launched, and each time a new scene is loaded, each interface controller has a lifecycle consisting of initialization, user interaction and termination. At multiple points within this lifecycle, calls are made to specific methods within the interface controller of the current scene thereby providing points within the code where initialization and de-initialization tasks can be performed.

Chapter 5

5. An Example Interactive WatchKit App

H aving covered actions and outlets in the previous chapter, it is now time to make practical use of these concepts. With this goal in mind, this chapter will work through the creation of a WatchKit app intended to demonstrate the way in which the Interface Builder and Assistant Editor features of Xcode work together to simplify the creation of actions and outlets to implement interactive behavior within a WatchKit app.

5.1 About the Example App

The purpose of the WatchKit app created in this chapter is to calculate a recommended gratuity amount when dining at a restaurant. A mechanism will be provided for the user to select the amount of the bill and then tap a button to display the recommended tip amount (assuming a percentage of 20%). Instead of selecting the option to include a WatchKit app when the project is created, this chapter will introduce the steps necessary to add a WatchKit app to an existing iOS app project.

5.2 Creating the TipCalcApp Project

Start Xcode and, on the Welcome screen, select the *Create a new Xcode project* option. On the template screen choose the *Application* option located under *iOS* in the left hand panel followed by *Single View Application* in the main panel. Click *Next,* set the product name to *TipCalcApp,* enter your organization identifier and make sure that the *Devices* menu is set to *Universal.* Before clicking *Next*, change the *Language* menu to Swift if necessary. On the final screen, choose a location in which to store the project files and click on the *Create* button to proceed to the main Xcode project window.

5.3 Adding the WatchKit App Target

For the purposes of this example we will assume that the iOS app has already been implemented. The next step, therefore, is to add the WatchKit app target to the project. Within Xcode, select the *File -> New -> Target...* menu option. In the target template dialog, select the *Application* option listed beneath the *watchOS* heading. In the main panel, select the *WatchKit App* icon and click on *Next.* On the subsequent screen (Figure 5-1) enter *TipCalcApp WatchKit App* into the Product Name field and turn off the *Include Glance Scene*, *Include Complication* and *Include Notification Scene* options before clicking on the *Finish* button:

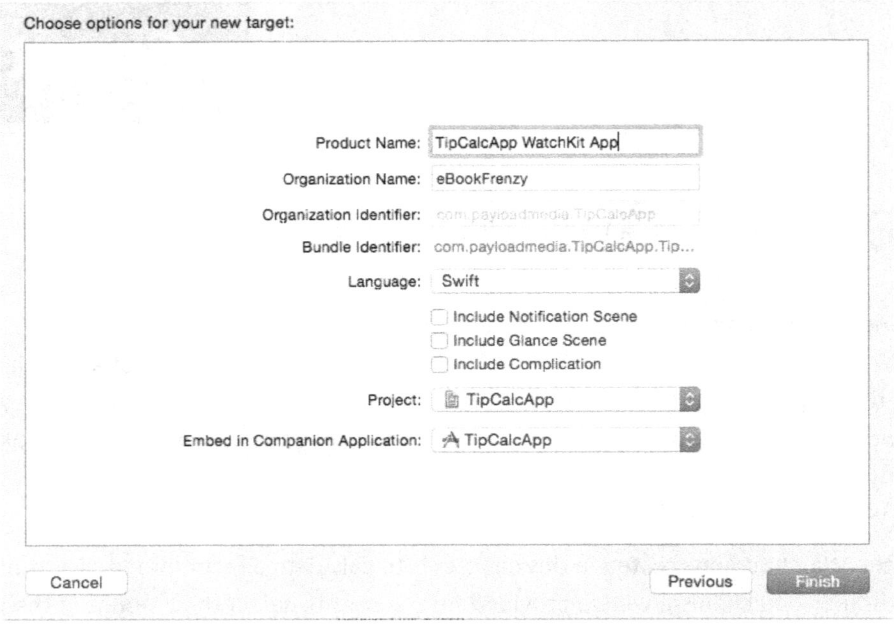

Figure 5-1

As soon as the extension target has been created, a new panel will appear requesting permission to activate the new scheme for the extension target. Activate this scheme now by clicking on the *Activate* button in the request panel.

5.4 Designing the WatchKit App User Interface

Within the Xcode Project Navigator panel unfold the *TipCalcApp WatchKit App* folder entry and select the *Interface.storyboard* file to load it into the Interface Builder tool.

The user interface for the app is going to consist of two Label objects, a Slider and a Button. Begin the design by locating the Label object in the Object Library panel and dragging and dropping it onto the scene so that it appears at the top of the scene layout. Select the newly added label and display the Attributes Inspector in the utilities panel (*View -> Utilities -> Show Attributes Inspector*). Within the inspector panel, change the text so that it reads $0.00 and change the Alignment setting so that the text is positioned in the center of the label.

Remaining within the Attributes Inspector panel, click on the 'T' icon located in the far right of the *Font* attribute text field to display the font setting panel. Within this panel, change the *Font* setting to *System*, the *Style* to *Bold* and the *Size* value to 28 as shown in Figure 5-2. Once the font settings are complete, click on the *Done* button to commit the changes.

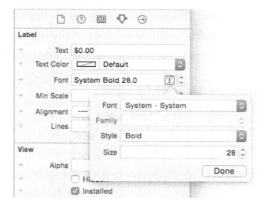

Figure 5-2

With the Label object still selected within the scene, locate the *Alignment* section within the Attribute Inspector panel and change the *Horizontal* property setting to *Center*.

Next, drag a Slider object from the library and drop it onto the scene so that it appears beneath the Label object. Select the Slider object in the scene and, within the Attributes Inspector, configure the *Minimum* and *Maximum* attributes to 0 and 100 respectively and enable the *Continuous* checkbox. Since we want the slider to adjust in $1 units the *Steps* value needs to be changed to 100.

Drag and drop a second Label object so that it is positioned beneath the slider. Select the new label and set the same alignment, font and positioning properties as those used for the first label. This time, however, change the *Text Color* attribute so that the text is displayed in green.

Finally, position a Button object beneath the second label. Double click on the button and change the text so it reads "Calculate Tip". With the button still selected, use the Attribute Inspector and change the *Vertical* property located in the *Alignment* section of the panel to *Bottom*.

At this point the scene layout should resemble that shown in Figure 5-3:

Figure 5-3

The user interface design is now complete. The next step is to configure outlets on the two Label objects so that the values displayed can be controlled from within the code of the interface controller class in the WatchKit extension. Before doing so, however, it is worth taking a look at the interface controller class file.

5.5 Reviewing the Interface Controller Class

As previously discussed, each scene within the storyboard of a WatchKit app has associated with it an interface controller class located within the WatchKit extension. By default, the Swift source code file for this class will be named *InterfaceController.swift* and will be located within the Project Navigator panel under the *<AppName> WatchKit Extension* folder where *<AppName>* is replaced by the name of the containing iOS app. Figure 5-4, for example, highlights the interface controller source file for the main scene of the TipCalcApp extension:

Figure 5-4

Locate and select this file so that it loads into the editing panel. Once loaded, the code should read as outlined in the following listing:

```
import WatchKit
import Foundation

class InterfaceController: WKInterfaceController {

    override func awakeWithContext(context: AnyObject?) {
        super.awakeWithContext(context)

        // Configure interface objects here.
    }

    override func willActivate() {
```

```
        // This method is called when watch view controller is about to be
visible to user
        super.willActivate()
    }

    override func didDeactivate() {
        // This method is called when watch view controller is no longer
 visible
        super.didDeactivate()
    }

}
```

Xcode has created an interface controller class implementation that overrides a subset of the lifecycle methods outlined in the chapter entitled *An Overview of WatchKit App Architecture*. Later in this chapter some initialization code will be added to the *willActivate()* method. At this point, some outlets need to be configured so that changes can be made to the Label objects in the main WatchKit app scene.

5.6 **Establishing Outlet Connections**

Outlets provide the interface controller class with access to the interface objects within the corresponding storyboard scene. Outlets can be created visually within Xcode by using Interface Builder and the Assistant Editor panel.

To establish outlets, begin by loading the *Interface.storyboard* file into the Interface Builder tool. Within Interface Builder, click on the scene so that it is highlighted before displaying the Assistant Editor by selecting the *View -> Assistant Editor -> Show Assistant Editor* menu option. Alternatively, it may also be displayed by selecting the center button (the one containing an image of interlocking circles) of the row of Editor toolbar buttons in the top right hand corner of the main Xcode window as illustrated in the following figure:

Figure 5-5

In the event that multiple Assistant Editor panels are required, additional tiles may be added using the *View -> Assistant Editor -> Add Assistant Editor* menu option.

By default, the editor panel will appear to the right of the main editing panel in the Xcode window. For example, in Figure 5-6 the panel to the immediate right of the Interface Builder panel is the Assistant Editor (marked A):

Figure 5-6

By default, the Assistant Editor will be in *Automatic* mode, whereby it automatically attempts to display the correct source file based on the currently selected item in Interface Builder. If the correct file is not displayed, use the toolbar along the top of the editor panel to select the correct file. The small instance of the Assistant Editor icon in this toolbar can be used to switch to *Manual* mode allowing the file to be selected from a pull-right menu containing all the source files in the project:

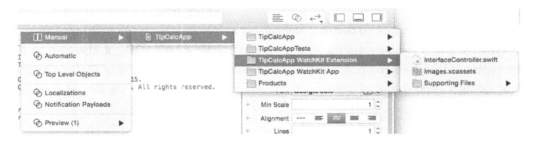

Figure 5-7

Make sure that the *InterfaceController.swift* file is displayed in the Assistant Editor and establish an outlet for the top-most label by Ctrl-clicking on the Label object in the scene and dragging the resulting line to the area immediately beneath the *class InterfaceController* declaration line in the Assistant Editor panel as shown in Figure 5-8:

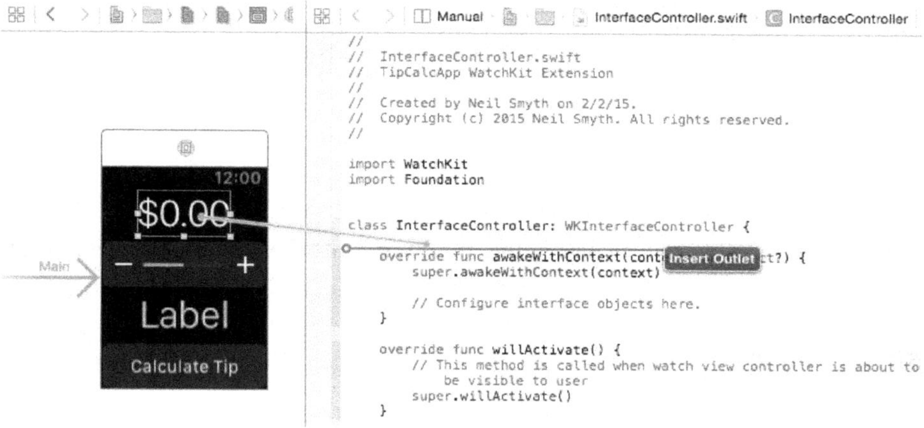

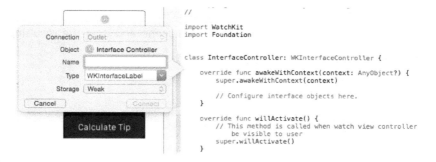

Figure 5-8

Upon releasing the line, the configuration panel illustrated in Figure 5-9 will appear requesting details about the outlet to be defined.

Figure 5-9

Since this is an outlet, the *Connection* menu should be set to *Outlet*. The type and storage values are also correct for this type of outlet. The only task that remains is to enter a name for the outlet, so in the *Name* field enter *amountLabel* before clicking on the *Connect* button.

Repeat the above steps to establish an outlet for the second Label object named *tipLabel*.

Once the connections have been established, review the *InterfaceController.swift* file and note that the outlet properties have been declared for us by the Assistant Editor:

```
import WatchKit
import Foundation

class InterfaceController: WKInterfaceController {
```

```
    @IBOutlet weak var amountLabel: WKInterfaceLabel!
    @IBOutlet weak var tipLabel: WKInterfaceLabel!
.
.
.
}
```

When we reference these outlet variables within the interface controller code we are essentially accessing the objects in the user interface.

5.7 Establishing Action Connections

Now that the outlets have been created, the next step is to connect the Slider and Button objects to action methods within the interface controller class. When the user increments or decrements the slider value the interface controller will need to change the value displayed on the *amountLabel* object to reflect the new value. This means that an action method will need to be implemented within the interface controller class and connected via an action to the Slider object in the storyboard scene.

With the scene displayed in Interface Builder and the *InterfaceController.swift* file loaded into the Assistant Editor panel, Ctrl-click on the Slider object in the storyboard scene and drag the resulting line to a position immediately beneath the *tipLabel* outlet as illustrated in Figure 5-10:

Figure 5-10

Once the line has been released, the connection configuration dialog will appear (Figure 5-11). Within the dialog, select *Action* from the *Connection* menu and enter *sliderChange* as the name of the action method to be called when the value of the slider is changed by the user:

Click on the *Connect* button to establish the action and note that Xcode has added a stub action method at the designated location within the *InterfaceController.swift* file:

```
import WatchKit
import Foundation

class InterfaceController: WKInterfaceController {

    @IBOutlet weak var amountLabel: WKInterfaceLabel!
    @IBOutlet weak var tipLabel: WKInterfaceLabel!

    @IBAction func sliderChange(value: Float) {
    }
.

.
}
```

An action method will also need to be called when the user taps the Button object in the user interface. Ctrl-click on the Button object in the scene and drag the resulting line to a position beneath the *sliderChange* method. On releasing the line, the connection dialog will appear once again. Change the connection menu to *Action* and enter *calculateTip* as the method name before clicking on the *Connect* button to create the connection.

5.8 Implementing the sliderChange Action Method

The Slider object added to the scene layout is actually an instance of the WatchKit framework WKInterfaceSlider class. When the user adjusts the slider value, that value is passed to the action method assigned to the object, in this instance the *sliderChange* method created in the previous section.

It is the responsibility of this action method to display the current value on the amount label using the *amountLabel* outlet variable and to store the current amount locally within the interface controller object so that it can be accessed when the user requests that the tip amount be calculated. Select the

InterfaceController.swift file and modify it to add a floating point variable in which to store the current slider value and to implement the code in the *sliderChange* method:

```
class InterfaceController: WKInterfaceController {

    @IBOutlet weak var amountLabel: WKInterfaceLabel!
    @IBOutlet weak var tipLabel: WKInterfaceLabel!

    var currentAmount: Float = 0.00

    @IBAction func sliderChange(value: Float) {
        let amountString = String(format: "%0.2f", value)
        amountLabel.setText("$\(amountString)")
        currentAmount = value
    }
    .
    .
    .
}
```

The code added to the action method performs a number of tasks. First a new String object is created based on the current floating point value passed to the action method from the Slider object. This is formatted to two decimal places to reflect dollars and cents. The *setText* method of the *amountLabel* outlet is then called to set the text displayed on the Label object in the user interface, prefixing the *amountString* with a dollar sign. Finally, the current value is assigned to the *currentAmount* variable where it can be accessed later from within the *calculateTip* action method.

Make sure that the run target in the Xcode toolbar is set to *TipCalcApp Watchkit App* and click on the run button to launch the app. Once it has loaded into the simulator, click on the − and + slider buttons to change the current value. Note that the amount label is updated each time the value changes:

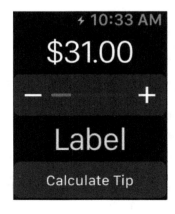

Figure 5-12

5.9 Implementing the calculateTip Action Method

The *calculateTip* action method will calculate 20% of the current amount and display the result to the user via the *tipAmount* outlet, once again using string formatting to display the result to two decimal places prefixed with a dollar sign:

```
@IBAction func calculateTip() {
    let tipAmount = currentAmount * 0.20
    let tipString = String(format: "%0.2f", tipAmount)
    tipLabel.setText("$\(tipString)")
}
```

Run the application once again, adjust the slider and click on the Calculate Tip button, verifying that the tip amount is displayed on the tip Label object as shown in Figure 5-13:

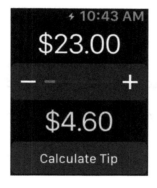

Figure 5-13

5.10 Hiding the Tip Label

Until the user taps the calculate button, the tip label is largely redundant. The final task for the project, therefore, is to hide the tip label until the app is ready to display the recommended tip amount. The Label object can be hidden by adding some code to the *willActivate* lifecycle method within the *InterfaceController.swift* class file as follows:

```
override func willActivate() {
    // This method is called when watch view controller is about to be
visible to user
    super.willActivate()
    tipLabel.setHidden(true)
}
```

This method uses the *tipLabel* outlet to call the *setHidden* method on the Label object so that it is hidden from the user. When an object is hidden it is invisible to the user and the user interface layout behaves as though the object no longer exists. As such, the layout will re-arrange to occupy the vacated space. To hide an object whilst retaining the occupied space, call the *setAlpha* method passing through a value of 0 to make the object transparent.

Having hidden the label during the initialization phase, a line of code needs to be added to the *calculateTip* method to reveal the Label object after the tip has been calculated:

```
@IBAction func calculateTip() {
    let tipAmount = currentAmount * 0.20
    let tipString = String(format: "%0.2f", tipAmount)
    tipLabel.setText("$\(tipString)")
    tipLabel.setHidden(false)
}
```

Run the app one last time and verify that the tip label remains hidden until the calculate button is pressed.

5.11 Removing the WatchKit App

To avoid cluttering the Apple Watch Home screen with all of the sample WatchKit apps created in this book, it is recommended that the apps be removed from the Apple Watch device at the end of each chapter.

One option is to delete the WatchKit app from the Apple Watch by pressing and holding on the app icon on the watch screen home screen until the "x" marker appears next to the app icons. Tapping the "x" will remove the WatchKit app from the Apple Watch.

Another option is to hide the app using the Apple Watch app. This app is installed by default on iPhone devices and is the app that you used when pairing your iPhone with the Apple Watch. Within this app, select the *My Watch* option in the bottom tab bar and scroll down and select the *TipCalcApp* entry. On the resulting preferences screen (Figure 5-14) turn off the *Show App on Apple Watch* option:

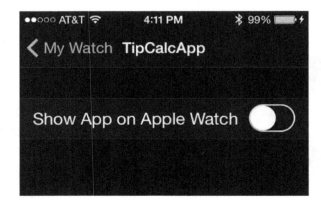

Figure 5-14

5.12 **Summary**

The Interface Builder tool and the Assistant Editor panel can be used together to quickly establish outlet and action connections between the user interface objects in a storyboard scene and the underlying interface controller scene in the WatchKit extension. This chapter has worked through the creation of a sample application project designed to demonstrate this technique. This chapter also made use of the *willActivate* lifecycle method to perform an initialization task and briefly covered the hiding and showing of objects in a WatchKit scene.

6. An Overview of WatchKit Tables

The WatchKit Table object allows content to be displayed within a WatchKit app scene in the form of a single vertical column of rows. Tables can be used purely as a mechanism for displaying lists of information, or to implement navigation whereby the selection of a particular row within a table triggers a transition to another scene within the storyboard.

This chapter will provide an overview of tables in WatchKit, exploring how tables are structured and explaining areas such as the WKInterfaceTable class, row controllers, row controller classes, row controller types and the steps necessary to initialize a WatchKit table at runtime. The next chapter, entitled *A WatchKit Table Tutorial*, will then work through the creation of an example WatchKit table scene. Table based navigation will then be explored in the *Implementing WatchKit Table Navigation* chapter of the book.

6.1 The WatchKit Table

WatchKit tables provide a way to display information to the user in the form of a single column of rows. If a table has too many rows to fit within the watch display the user can scroll up and down within the table using the touch screen or the Digital Crown. The individual rows in a table may also be configured to call action methods when tapped by the user.

Tables are represented by the WatchKit WKInterfaceTable class, with each row displayed within the table represented by a *table row controller* instance.

6.2 Table Row Controller

There are two parts to the table row controller. The first is the visual representation of the row within the table. This essentially defines which user interface objects are to be displayed in the row (for example a row might consist of an Image and a Label object).

The second component of a table row is a corresponding *row controller class* which resides within the WatchKit app extension. This class is created as a subclass of the NSObject class and, at a minimum, contains outlets to the user interface objects contained in the row controller. Once declared, these outlets are used by the scene's interface controller to configure the content displayed within each row. If the row controller in the scene contained two Label objects, for example, the outlets could be used to set the text on those labels for each row in the table.

6.3 **Row Controller Type**

The user interface objects defined within a row controller in the scene combined with the corresponding row controller class in the extension define the *row controller type*. A single table can consist of multiple row controller types. One row controller might, for example, contain a label and an image while another might contain two labels. The type of row controller used for each row within the table is controlled by the interface controller during the table row initialization process.

6.4 **Table Row Initialization**

When a scene containing a table is displayed within a WatchKit app, the table object will need a row controller instance for each row to be displayed to the user. The interface controller is responsible for performing the following initialization tasks:

1. Calculate the number of rows to be displayed in the table.
2. Request the creation of a row controller instance of a particular row controller type for each row in the table.
3. Configure the appearance of the user interface objects in each row using the outlets declared in the row controller class.

6.5 **Implementing a Table in a WatchKit App Scene**

A Table is added to a WatchKit scene by dragging and dropping a Table object from the Object Library onto the storyboard scene. By default, the table instance will contain a single row controller instance containing a Group object. A Group object is a single user interface element that can contain one or more interface objects in a horizontal or vertical arrangement. Figure 6-1 shows a scene with a newly added table with the default row controller:

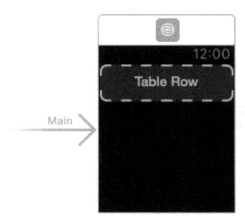

Figure 6-1

The hierarchical structure of the table and table row controller can be viewed within the Xcode *Document Outline* panel. This panel appears by default to the left of the Interface Builder panel and is controlled by the small button in the bottom left hand corner (indicated by the arrow in Figure 6-2) of the Interface Builder panel.

Figure 6-2

When displayed, the document outline shows a hierarchical overview of the elements that make up a user interface layout. This enables us, for example, to see that a scene consists of a Table, Table Row Controller and a Group object:

Figure 6-3

The row controller within the table is a template for the row controllers that will be created within the interface controller. To design the row, simply drag and drop user interface objects from the Object Library onto the row and resize the items to achieve the desired layout. In Figure 6-4, for example, the template row controller contains an image and label:

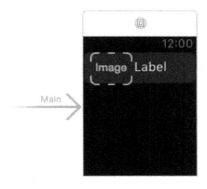

Figure 6-4

It is important to be aware that the appearance of the visual elements in a row is generally defined at runtime by the interface controller using the outlets declared in the row controller class. Any attributes set within the storyboard will serve as the default attributes for the visual elements and will appear in the app at runtime unless overridden in the interface controller.

The row controller template must also be assigned an identifier which will be referenced in the interface controller code when instances of that row type are created during initialization. The identifier is configured by selecting the row controller item in the Document Outline panel and entering a suitable identifier name into the Identifier field of the Attributes Inspector panel:

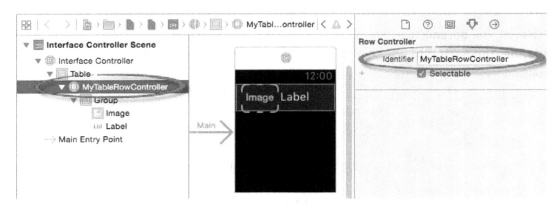

Figure 6-5

6.6 Adding the Row Controller Class to the Extension

As previously outlined, each row controller type must have a corresponding row controller class file within the app extension. This must be a subclass of NSObject and can be created using the following steps:

1. Locate the WatchKit Extension folder within the Project Navigator panel and Ctrl-click on it.
2. From the resulting menu select the *New File...* menu option.
3. In the new file template panel, select *Source* listed under *watchOS* in the left hand panel and *WatchKit Class* from the main panel before clicking *Next*.
4. Enter a name for the class into the *Class* field and select *NSObject* from the *Subclass of:* menu before clicking *Next*.
5. Click *Finish* to add the new class to the extension.

6.7 Associating a Row Controller with a Row Controller Class

Before the table can be displayed, the row controller in the scene needs to be associated with the corresponding row controller class residing within the extension. This is achieved by selecting the row controller in the Document Outline panel, displaying the Identity Inspector (*View -> Utilities -> Show Identity Inspector*) and selecting the row controller class name from the *Class* menu.

6.8 **Creating Table Rows at Runtime**

The interface controller class for the scene containing the table is responsible for configuring the table and creating the rows during the initialization phase of the WatchKit app launch process. The interface controller will need an outlet connected to the table instance in the scene on which it will call either the *setNumberOfRows(_:withRowType:)* or *setRowTypes(_:)* methods:

- **setNumberOfRows** – Used when all of the rows to be created in the table are of the same row type. This method takes as parameters the number of rows to be created and the Identifier string for the row controller type as defined in the Attributes Inspector.
- **setRowTypes** – Called when the table is to comprise rows of different types. This method takes as a parameter an array containing the Identifiers of the row controller types (as defined in the Attributes Inspector) in the order in which they are to appear in the table.

When the above methods are called they remove any existing rows from the table and create new rows based on the parameters provided. The methods also create an internal array containing an instance of the row controller class for each of the rows displayed in the table. These instances can then be accessed by calling the *rowControllerAtIndex* method of the table object. Once a reference to a row controller class instance has been obtained, the outlets declared in that instance can be used to set the attributes of the user interface objects in the row controller.

The following code listing, for example, displays a color name on each row of a table within a WatchKit app scene using the row type identified by "MyTableRowController":

```
import WatchKit
import Foundation

class InterfaceController: WKInterfaceController {

    // The outlet to the Table object in the scene
    @IBOutlet weak var myTable: WKInterfaceTable!

    // The data array
    let colorNames = ["Red", "Green", "Blue", "Yellow"]

    override init() {
        super.init()
        loadTable() // Call to initialize the table rows
    }

    func loadTable() {
        // Create the table row controller instances
```

```
                    // based on the number of items in colorNames array
                    myTable.setNumberOfRows(colorNames.count,
                            withRowType: "MyTableRowController")

                    // Iterate through each of the table row controller
                    // class instances.
                    for (index, labelText) in enumerate(colorNames)
                    {
                        // Get a reference to the current instance
                        let row = myTable.rowControllerAtIndex(index)
                                as MyRowController
                        // Set the text using the outlet in the row controller
                        // class instance.
                        row.myLabel.setText(labelText)
                    }
                }
            .
            .
            .
        }
```

This approach is not restricted to the initialization phase of a table. The same technique can be used to dynamically change the properties of the user interface objects in a table row at any point when a table is displayed during the lifecycle of an app. The following action method, for example, dynamically changes the text displayed on the label in row zero of the table initialized in the above code:

```
@IBAction func buttonTap() {
    let row = myTable.rowControllerAtIndex(0) as MyRowController
    row.myLabel.setText("Hello")
}
```

6.9 Inserting Table Rows

Additional rows may be added to a table at runtime using the *insertRowsAtIndexes* method of the table instance. This method takes as parameters an index set indicating the positions at which the rows are to be inserted and the identifier of the row controller type to be used. The following code, for example, inserts new rows of type "MyImageRowController" at row index positions 0, 2 and 4:

```
let indexSet = NSMutableIndexSet()
indexSet.addIndex(0)
indexSet.addIndex(2)
indexSet.addIndex(4)

myTable.insertRowsAtIndexes(indexSet,
```

```
        withRowType: "MyImageRowController")
```

6.10 **Removing Table Rows**

Similarly, rows may be removed from a table using the *removeRowsAtIndexes* method of the table instance, once again passing through as a parameter an index set containing the rows to be removed. The following code, for example, removes the rows inserted in the above code fragment:

```
let indexSet = NSMutableIndexSet()
indexSet.addIndex(0)
indexSet.addIndex(2)
indexSet.addIndex(4)

myTable.removeRowsAtIndexes(indexSet)
```

6.11 **Scrolling to a Specific Table Row**

The table can be made to scroll to a specific row programmatically using the *scrollToRowAtIndex* method of the table instance, passing through as a parameter an integer value representing the index position of the destination row:

```
myTable.scrollToRowAtIndex(1)
```

A negative index value will scroll to the top of the table, while a value greater than the last index position will scroll to the end.

6.12 **Summary**

Tables are created in WatchKit using the WKInterfaceTable class which allows content to be presented to the user in the form of a single column of rows. Each row within a table is represented visually within a storyboard scene by a row controller which, in turn, has a corresponding row controller class residing in the app extension. A single table can display multiple row controller types so that individual rows in a table can comprise different user interface objects. Initialization and runtime configuration of the row controller instances is the responsibility of the interface controller for the scene in which the table appears. A variety of methods are available on the table class to dynamically insert and remove rows while the table is displayed to the user.

7. A WatchKit Table Tutorial

The previous chapter provided an overview of tables within WatchKit apps. Now that these basics have been covered, this chapter will provide a tutorial that implements a table-based user interface within a WatchKit app using the techniques outlined in the previous chapter.

7.1 About the Table Example

The WatchKit app created in this chapter will take the form of an extension to a hypothetical iOS-based physical fitness application. The main WatchKit app storyboard will use a table to provide a list of the different steps in a workout routine with each table row containing an image and a label.

Although no interactive features will be added to the app in this chapter, the example will be extended in the next chapter (*Implementing WatchKit Table Navigation*) so that selecting a row in the table navigates to a second scene providing more detail on the selected workout step.

7.2 Creating the Table Project

Start Xcode and create a new iOS project. On the template screen choose the *Application* option located under *watchOS* in the left hand panel and select *iOS App with WatchKit App*. Click *Next*, set the product name to *TableDemoApp*, enter your organization identifier and make sure that the *Devices* menu is set to *Universal*. Before clicking *Next*, change the *Language* menu to Swift and turn off all of the *Include* options. On the final screen, choose a location in which to store the project files and click on *Create* to proceed to the main Xcode project window.

7.3 Adding the Table to the Scene

Navigate to and select the storyboard file for the WatchKit app (*TableDemoApp WatchKit App -> Interface.storyboard*) so that it appears in the Interface Builder tool. Within the Object Library panel, locate the Table object and drag and drop it onto the scene layout so that it appears as shown in Figure 7-1:

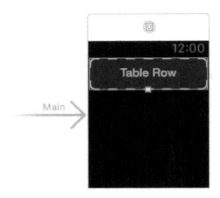

Figure 7-1

Drag an Image object from the Object Library panel and drop it onto the table row in the storyboard scene so that it is positioned on the left hand side of the row. Repeat this step, this time selecting a Label object and positioning it to the right of the Image object. Select the label and, using the Attributes Inspector panel, set the *Vertical* Alignment menu to *Center*.

Select the Image object and make the following changes within the Attributes Inspector panel:

1. Set the *Mode* menu to *Aspect Fit* so that images are not distorted when displayed.
2. In the Alignment section of the panel change the *Vertical* menu to *Center* so that the image is in alignment with the label object.
3. Within the Size section of the panel set both the *Height* and *Width* attributes to be *Fixed* at 25 points.

On completion of these steps, the layout of the scene should resemble that of Figure 7-2:

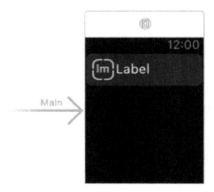

Figure 7-2

Display the Document Outline panel, select the Table Row Controller object from the hierarchy, display the Attributes Inspector panel and enter "MyRowController" into the *Identifier* field (Figure 7-3):

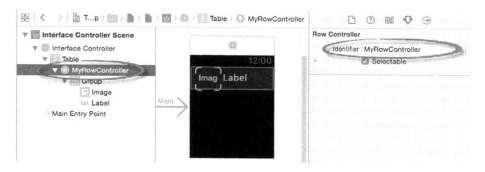

Figure 7-3

7.4 Creating the Row Controller Class

As discussed in the chapter entitled *An Overview of WatchKit Tables*, each row controller in the table must have associated with it a row controller class within the app extension. The next step, therefore, is to add this class. Locate the *TableDemoApp WatchKit Extension* entry with in the Project Navigator panel and Ctrl-click on it to display the context menu. From this menu, select the *New File…* menu option and, in the template selection panel, click on the *Source* entry listed under *watchOS* in the left hand panel and *WatchKit Class* from the main panel. Click *Next* to proceed to the next screen, enter MyRowController into the *Class* field and select *NSObject* from the *Subclass of:* menu as outlined in Figure 7-4:

Figure 7-4

Click *Next* followed by *Create* to generate the source file for the class into the WatchKit app extension folder.

Before connecting outlets from the storyboard scene to the new row controller class, the row controller needs to be configured as a subclass of MyRowController. With the *Interface.storyboard* file selected and the Document Outline visible select the row controller object and display the Identity Inspector panel (*View ->*

Utilities -> Show Identity Inspector). Within the Identity Inspector panel, use the *Class* drop down menu to select the *MyRowController* class as shown in Figure 7-5:

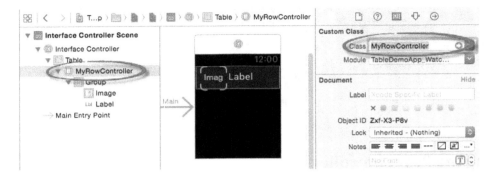

Figure 7-5

7.5 Establishing the Outlets

With the row controller class created, it is now time to establish the outlets for the image and label objects containing the row controller in the storyboard scene. Select the *Interface.storyboard* file so that it loads into Interface Builder, select the image object and display the Assistant Editor panel using the button displaying interlocking rings in the Xcode toolbar:

Figure 7-6

Once the Assistant Editor has appeared, verify that it has loaded the *MyRowController.swift* file. In the event that it has not loaded the correct file, use the toolbar along the top of the editor panel to select the correct file. The small instance of the Assistant Editor icon in this toolbar can be used to switch to Manual mode allowing the file to be selected from a pull-right menu containing all the source files in the project. From this menu, select *Manual -> TableDemoApp -> TableDemoApp Watchkit Extension -> MyRowController.swift*.

Figure 7-7

With the *MyRowController.swift* file displayed in the Assistant Editor panel, Ctrl-click on the image object in the storyboard scene and drag the resulting line to a location beneath the class declaration line in the Assistant Editor panel. Release the line and establish an outlet connection named *myImage*.

Repeat the above step to establish an outlet from the Label object named *myLabel*. On completion of these steps, the *MyRowController.swift* file should read as follows:

```
import WatchKit

class MyRowController: NSObject {

    @IBOutlet weak var myImage: WKInterfaceImage!
    @IBOutlet weak var myLabel: WKInterfaceLabel!
}
```

With these steps completed, the next step is to create some data to be displayed and to add initialization code to the interface controller to display the rows at runtime.

7.6 Connecting the Table Outlet

In the course of initializing the table it will be necessary to access the table instance from within the interface controller class which will, in turn, require the establishment of an outlet. With the *Interface.storyboard* file selected and the Document Outline panel displayed, open the Assistant Editor panel and make sure that it is displaying the content of the *InterfaceController.swift* file. Ctrl-click on the *Table* entry in the Document Outline panel and drag the resulting line to a position immediately beneath the class declaration line in the Assistant Editor panel:

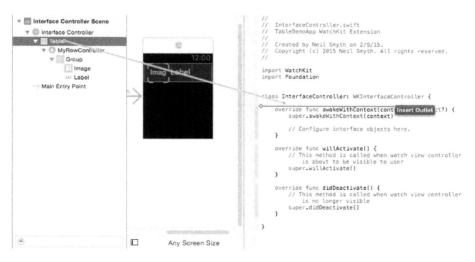

Figure 7-8

Release the line and establish an outlet named *myTable* in the resulting connection dialog.

7.7 Creating the Data

Clearly the rows within the table consist of an image and a label. The next step is to add some data to the project to serve as content for these two objects. This will take the form of two arrays declared within the interface controller class consisting of the names of the image files to be displayed on the Image object and strings to display on the Label object. Select the *InterfaceController.swift* file and edit it to add these two arrays as follows:

```
import WatchKit
import Foundation


class InterfaceController: WKInterfaceController {

    @IBOutlet weak var myTable: WKInterfaceTable!

    let stringData = ["Warm-up", "Cardio", "Weightlifting", "Core", "Bike",
"Cooldown"]

    let imageData = ["walking", "treadmill", "weights", "core",
"bikeriding", "cooldown"]
    .
    .
    .
}
```

Next, a method needs to be added to the class to initialize the table with the content of the data arrays. Remaining within the *InterfaceController.swift* file, implement this method as follows:

```
func loadTable() {

    myTable.setNumberOfRows(stringData.count,
            withRowType: "MyRowController")

    for (index, labelText) in stringData.enumerate() {
        let row = myTable.rowControllerAtIndex(index)
            as! MyRowController
        row.myLabel.setText(labelText)
        row.myImage.setImage(UIImage(named: imageData[index]))
    }
}
```

The method identifies the number of elements in the string array and uses that value to set the number of rows within the table while specifying the row type as MyRowController. The code then iterates through each row in the table setting image and label properties using the two arrays as the data sources for the content to be displayed.

The *init* lifecycle method now needs to be overridden and implemented to call the new *loadTable* method when the scene loads within the WatchKit app. Add this method to the *InterfaceController.swift* file so that it reads as follows:

```
override init() {
    super.init()
    loadTable()
}
```

7.8 Adding the Image Files to the Project

The final task before testing the app is to add the image files referenced in the imageData array. These are contained within the *fitness_icons* folder of the sample code download which may be obtained from the following URL:

http://www.ebookfrenzy.com/print/watchos2/index.php

Within the code Project Navigator panel, select the *Assets.xcassets* entry listed under the *TableDemoApp WatchKit App Extension* folder so that the asset catalog panel appears. Ctrl-click in the left hand panel of the asset catalog and select the *Import...* option from the resulting menu:

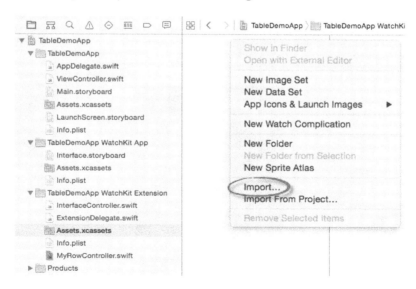

Figure 7-9

In the file import selection panel, navigate to and select the *fitness_icons* folder before clicking on the *Open* button. The images will be imported into the asset catalog as an image set named *fitness_icons* as shown in Figure 7-10:

Figure 7-10

7.9 Testing the WatchKit App

Select the current scheme in the toolbar and use the drop down menu (Figure 7-11) to select the *TableDemoApp WatchKit App -> iPhone 6 + Apple Watch – 38mm* option:

Figure 7-11

With the correct build scheme and run target selected, click on the run button to launch the app on the simulator where it should appear as illustrated in Figure 7-12:

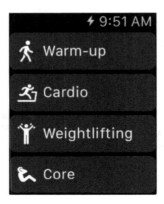

Figure 7-12

Assuming that the app runs as expected, note that it is possible to scroll through the rows but that selecting a row has no effect beyond some shadowing indicating that the row was selected. This functionality will be added in the chapter entitled *Implementing WatchKit Table Navigation*.

7.10 **Adding a Title Row to the Table**

The project will now be extended to demonstrate the steps involved in displaying multiple row controller types within a WatchKit app table. For the purposes of this project this will involve the addition of a title row to the top of the table.

The first step is to add another row controller to the table. Begin by selecting the *Interface.storyboard* file and displaying the Document Outline panel. Within the Document Outline panel, select the My Table entry, display the Attributes Inspector and set the *Prototype Rows* property to 2 as outlined in Figure 7-13:

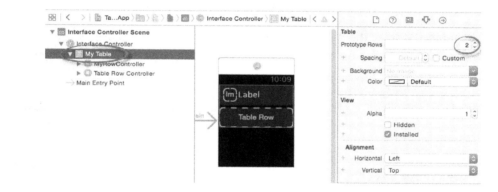

Figure 7-13

Drag a Label from the Object Library panel and drop it onto the new table row within the storyboard scene. With the new label selected, display the Attributes Inspector panel and set both the *Horizontal* and *Vertical* Alignment attributes to *Center.* On completion of these steps the scene should match that shown in Figure 7-14:

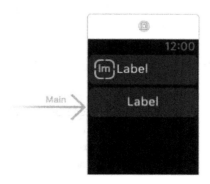

Figure 7-14

In the Document Outline panel, select the new *Table Row Controller* entry and enter *MyTitleRowController* into the Identifier field in the Attributes Inspector panel. Since this is a title row and is not intended to be selectable by the user, turn off the *Selectable* attribute.

As with the first row controller, this new controller will need a corresponding row controller class within the app extension. Locate and Ctrl-click on the *TableDemoApp WatchKit Extension* entry and select the *New File...* option from the menu. Repeat the steps performed earlier in this chapter to add a new WatchKit class named *MyTitleRowController* subclassed from NSObject.

7.11 **Connecting the Outlet and Initializing the Second Table Row**

Load the *Interface.storyboard* file into Interface Builder and display the Document Outline and Identity Inspector panels. In the Document Outline panel, select the MyTitleRowController entry and, from the Class menu in the Identity Inspector, select the newly created MyTitleRowController class.

Select the title Label object, display the Assistant Editor and make sure that it is displaying the content of the *MyTitleRowController.swift* file. Following the usual steps, establish an outlet for the Label object in the second row named *titleLabel.*

Finally, edit the *InterfaceController.swift* file and re-write the *loadTable* method so that it reads as follows:

```
func loadTable() {

    myTable.setRowTypes(["MyTitleRowController",
        "MyRowController",
        "MyRowController",
        "MyRowController",
        "MyRowController",
        "MyRowController",
        "MyRowController"])

    let titleRow = myTable.rowControllerAtIndex(0)
            as! MyTitleRowController

    titleRow.titleLabel.setText("Workout Plan")

    for index in 0..<stringData.count {
        let row = myTable.rowControllerAtIndex(index+1)
                    as! MyRowController
        row.myLabel.setText(stringData[index])
        row.myImage.setImage(UIImage(named: imageData[index]))
    }

}
```

This time, the method is calling the *setRowTypes* method of the table and passing through an array containing the identifier of the title row and six instances of the MyRowController row type. This will ensure that the first row is the title row.

Next, the code obtains a reference to the title row at index position 0 in the table's internal array and sets a string value on the text property that reads "Workout Plan". Finally, the method iterates through the remaining rows configuring the properties of the Image and Label objects accordingly.

Compile and run the app once again, noting that the title row now appears at the top of the table:

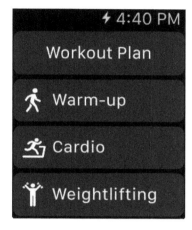

Figure 7-15

7.12 Summary

This chapter has worked through the creation of a project designed to demonstrate the steps involved in creating a table-based scene within a WatchKit app. Topics covered included the creation of a table scene, implementation of the supporting classes in the app extension and the process of supporting multiple row controller types within a single table.

8. Implementing WatchKit Table Navigation

The previous chapter introduced the concept of tables within WatchKit app scenes. An area of WatchKit tables that has been mentioned but not yet explored in detail involves the use of tables to implement navigation between storyboard scenes. This chapter will provide an overview of table based navigation (also referred to as hierarchical navigation) within WatchKit apps. Once the basics have been covered, the TableDemoApp project from the previous chapter will be extended to add navigation support.

8.1 Table Navigation in WatchKit Apps

Table based navigation allows an app to transition from one scene to another scene when a row within a table is selected by the user. When a table row is selected, the *didSelectRow* method of the interface controller associated with the current scene is called and passed a reference to the table object in which the selection took place together with an integer representing the index value of the selected row. It is then the responsibility of this method to perform the steps necessary to transition to the next scene.

8.2 Performing a Scene Transition

When implementing navigation-based behavior in a WatchKit app, each scene still has a corresponding interface controller. As the user navigates through scenes, the app framework maintains an internal navigation stack of the interface controllers. When a new scene is displayed it is *pushed* onto the navigation stack and becomes the currently active controller. The framework also places a left pointing chevron in the upper left hand corner (Figure 8-1) of the newly displayed scene which, when tapped, returns to the previous scene. When this happens, the current interface controller is *popped* off the stack and the interface controller beneath it moved to the top becoming the currently active and visible controller. In addition to the user tapping the chevron, a return to the previous scene may also be achieved programmatically via a call to the *popController* method of the current interface controller instance.

Figure 8-1

The interface controller for the first scene to be pushed onto the navigation stack is referred to as the *root interface controller*.

This stack based approach enables multiple levels of navigation to be implemented allowing the user to navigate back and forth through many scene levels. In this scenario it is also possible to trigger navigation back to the root interface controller, skipping all intermediate scenes in the navigation stack, via a call to the *popToRootController* method of the current interface controller instance.

The transition from one scene to another is initiated via a call to the *pushControllerWithName* method. This method takes as parameters the identifier name of the destination interface controller and an optional context object. The context object can be an object of any type and is intended to provide the destination interface controller with any data necessary to configure the new scene appropriate to the context of the selected row.

The *pushControllerWithName* method will initialize the destination interface controller and pass the context object through as a parameter to the controller's *awakeWithContext* lifecycle method.

8.3 Extending the TableDemoApp Project

In the remainder of this chapter, the TableDemoApp project will be extended so that when rows are selected within the table the app will transition to a second scene in which additional information about the selected item will be displayed. The first step in this tutorial is to add an additional scene and interface controller to the project to act as the detail scene.

8.4 Adding the Detail Scene to the Storyboard

Begin by launching Xcode and opening the TableDemoApp project created in the previous chapter. Once loaded, select the *Interface.storyboard* file so that it appears within the Interface Builder tool. The storyboard should currently consist of a single scene containing the table implementation. Add a second scene to the storyboard by locating the Interface Controller object in the Object Library panel and dragging and dropping it so that it is positioned to the right of the existing scene.

The detailed information about the selected workout step will be displayed on the second scene using a Label object so drag and drop a Label object from the Object Library onto the second scene. Once these steps have been performed the storyboard should resemble Figure 8-2:

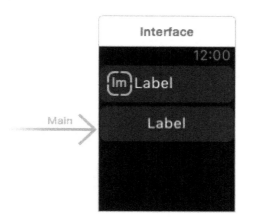

Figure 8-2

With the new scene added to the storyboard and selected so it is highlighted in blue, display the Attributes Inspector and enter "DetailInterfaceController" into the Identifier field.

By default, labels are configured to display a single line of text which will be clipped if the text exceeds the width of the watch display. To avoid this problem, configure the label to wrap the text over multiple lines by selecting the label in the second scene, displaying the Attributes Inspector and increasing the *Lines* attribute to 5.

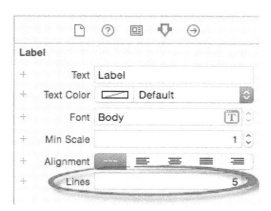

Figure 8-3

The design of the second scene is now complete. The next step is to add an interface controller to go with it.

8.5 Adding the Detail Interface Controller

Add the interface controller for the detail scene by locating the *TableDemoApp WatchKit Extension* entry in the Xcode Project Navigator panel, Ctrl-clicking on it and selecting *New File...* from the menu. In the template panel select the options to create a watchOS WatchKit Class source file and click *Next.* Name the new class *DetailInterfaceController* and configure it to be a subclass of WKInterfaceController. Click *Next,* make sure that the file is to be generated into the extension folder then click *Create.*

Load the *Interface.storyboard* file into Interface Builder. Select the second scene so that it highlights in blue, display the Identity Inspector panel and change the *Class* menu setting to the new *DetailInterfaceController* class as illustrated in Figure 8-4:

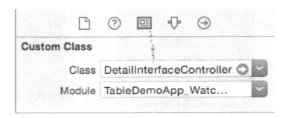

Figure 8-4

Select the Label object in the detail scene in the storyboard and display the Assistant Editor panel. Make sure that the Assistant Editor is displaying the *DetailInterfaceController.swift* file and then control click and drag from the Label object to a position just beneath the class declaration line in the Assistant Editor panel. Release the line and configure an outlet for the label named *detailLabel.* The outlet should now be declared within the class file as follows:

```
import WatchKit
import Foundation

class DetailInterfaceController: WKInterfaceController {

    @IBOutlet weak var detailLabel: WKInterfaceLabel!

    override func awakeWithContext(context: AnyObject?) {
        super.awakeWithContext(context)

        // Configure interface objects here.
    }
```

```
}
```

8.6 Adding the Detail Data Array

When the user selects a row in the table the detail scene will appear on the display. The label within this scene is intended to provide a more detailed explanation of the exercise to be performed. The text displayed will depend on which row was selected by the user. In other words, when the user selects the "Warm-up" row, the detail scene will provide details on how the user should perform the warm-up routine. For the purposes of this example, the array containing the detailed descriptions will be placed in the interface controller of the first scene. The appropriate text will then be extracted from the array based on the row chosen by the user and passed through to the detail view controller as the context object.

Select the *InterfaceController.swift* file and modify it to add the detailData array as follows:

```swift
import WatchKit
import Foundation

class InterfaceController: WKInterfaceController {

    @IBOutlet weak var myTable: WKInterfaceTable!


    let stringData = ["Warm-up", "Cardio", "Weightlifting", "Core", "Bike",
"Cooldown"]

    let imageData = ["walking", "treadmill", "weights", "core",
"bikeriding", "cooldown"]

    let detailData = ["Walk at a moderate pace for 20 minutes keeping heart
rate below 110.",
        "Run for 30 minutes keeping heart rate between 130 and 140.",
        "Perform 3 sets of 10 repetitions increasing weight by 5lb on each
set.",
        "Perform 2 sets of 20 crunches.",
        "Ride bike at moderate pace for 20 minutes.",
        "Walk for 10 minutes then stretch for 5 minutes."]
    .
    .
    .
}
```

8.7 **Implementing the didSelectRow Method**

As previously discussed, the selection of a row within a table (assuming that the row has been configured as being selectable) results in a call to the *didSelectRow* method within the corresponding interface controller instance. This method now needs to be added to the *InterfaceController.swift* file as follows:

```
override func table(table: WKInterfaceTable, didSelectRowAtIndex rowIndex:
Int) {
    pushControllerWithName("DetailInterfaceController",
        context: detailData[rowIndex-1])
}
```

The code within this method simply calls the *pushControllerWithName* method passing through as a parameter the Identifier of the interface controller to be displayed (in this case our DetailInterfaceController scene). The code also extracts the string from the detailData array based on the number of the row selected by the user. The first element in the array is at index position zero while the first selectable row in the table is row 1 due to the presence of the title row. Consequently, the rowIndex value is decremented by one to compensate.

Run the application and test that selecting a row transitions to the detail scene. The next step is to add some code to display the detail text on the label of the detail scene.

8.8 **Modifying the awakeWithContext Method**

The *awakeWithContext* method is one of the lifecycle methods called on an interface controller during the app initialization process. The parameter passed to the method when it is called is the context object referenced in the *pushControllerWithName* method call. Code now needs to be added to the *awakeWithContext* method within the DetailInterfaceController class file to display the context string via the *detailText* outlet. Select the *DetailInterfaceController.swift* file, locate the *awakeWithContext* method and modify it so it reads as follows:

```
override func awakeWithContext(context: AnyObject?) {
    super.awakeWithContext(context)
    detailLabel.setText(context as? String)
}
```

Compile and run the app once again and verify that selecting a row transitions to the detail scene and that the label displays the text that corresponds to the chosen row:

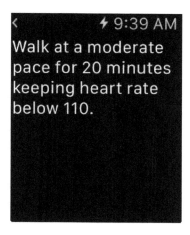

Figure 8-5

8.9 Adjusting the Interface Controller Insets

Although the text is displayed on the Label object in the detail scene, it appears a little too close to the outer edges of the display. The scene would probably be more visually appealing with a margin of some sort around the label content. This can be achieved by increasing the inset values on the interface controller. Modify these attributes by selecting the DetailInterfaceController object in the storyboard scene. This object can be selected by clicking on the black background of the scene, or via the Document Outline panel. Once selected, display the Attributes Inspector panel and change the *Insets* menu from *Default* to *Custom* to display the range of inset settings options. Set all four inset options to 5 as shown in Figure 8-6:

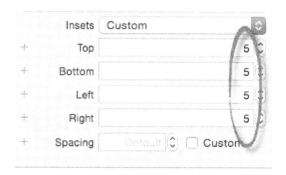

Figure 8-6

Re-run the app once again and verify that the label is now indented within the detail scene:

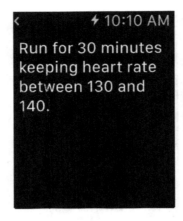

Figure 8-7

8.10 **Summary**

The WatchKit table provides an ideal starting point for providing a range of scene navigation options to the user. This chapter has extended the TableDemoApp project to implement navigation from the main scene to a detail scene. This example demonstrated the addition of new scenes to a storyboard and the passing of context data from one interface controller to another during a scene transition. The chapter also explored the use of insets to place a margin around the content of a scene.

Chapter 9

9. WatchKit Page-based User Interfaces and Modal Interface Controllers

The WatchKit framework provides the infrastructure to create what Apple refers to as page-based interfaces within WatchKit Apps. A page-based interface consists of two or more WatchKit scenes through which the user is able to navigate by making left and right swiping motions on the Apple Watch screen.

Another form of transition between scenes involves the modal presentation of interface controller scenes within a WatchKit app. Since the modal interface controller is a useful mechanism for transitioning to an interface controller from a page-based scene, both topics will be covered in this chapter.

9.1 The Elements of a Page-based WatchKit Interface

A page-based WatchKit interface provides a way to navigate through a sequence of scenes by making left and right swiping motions on the display. Each scene within the navigation sequence is represented by a dot along the bottom edge of the display with the dot representing the currently displayed scene highlighted. Figure 9-1, for example, shows a page-based interface containing three scenes in which the third scene is currently displayed:

Figure 9-1

When implementing page-based navigation, each scene will typically be assigned its own unique interface controller. As will be demonstrated in the next chapter, however, it also is possible to make use of context data to configure multiple scenes to use the same interface controller class.

9.2 Associating Page Scenes

The scenes that are to be collected into a page-based navigation interface are connected together using *next page* segues within the WatchKit app storyboard file. Segues are transitions that have been configured between one scene and another within a storyboard and are typically implemented within the Interface Builder environment. Consider, for example, a storyboard containing two scenes. A segue between the two scenes can be created within Interface Builder by Ctrl-clicking on the first scene and dragging the resulting line to the second scene as shown in Figure 9-2.

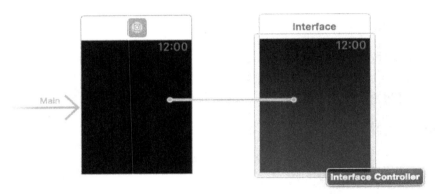

Figure 9-2

Upon releasing the line, a menu will appear providing a list of segue types available based on the context of the scene selections. Figure 9-3, for example, shows the segue menu providing the option to create a *next page* relationship segue between two scenes.

Figure 9-3

Once a segue has been established, it appears as a line and arrow between the two connected scenes (Figure 9-4). As with other items within a storyboard, a segue line can be selected and deleted. Certain types of segue may also be selected and given an identifier which, as will be shown later in the chapter, can be used to provide context during the transition from one scene to another.

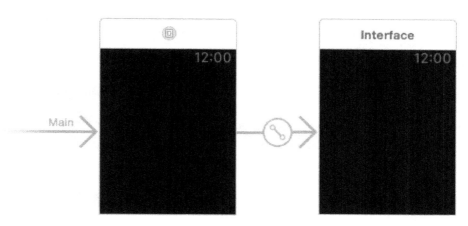

Figure 9-4

9.3 Managing Pages at Runtime

The interface controllers and ordering sequence for a paging interface may also be specified from within the application code via a call to the *reloadRootControllersWithNames* WKInterfaceController class method, passing through an array containing the identifiers of the interface controllers to be included in the page navigation together with a second array containing context data to be passed to each controller during scene transitions, for example:

```
WKInterfaceController.reloadRootControllersWithNames(
        ["controllerOne", "controllerTwo"],
           contexts: [contextObj1, contextObj2])
```

It is also possible to make an interface controller the currently displayed controller within the page sequence via a call to the *becomeCurrentPage* method within an initialization method of the interface controller to be displayed.

9.4 Modal Presentation of Interface Controllers

Interface controller scenes can be displayed modally using either storyboard segues, or programmatically from within a WatchKit app extension. Modal interface controllers are typically used to display information to the user and result in the scene associated with the controller appearing to the user together with an option located in the top left hand corner to dismiss the scene and return to the previous controller.

9.5 **Modal Presentation in Code**

Modal interface controllers can be displayed individually, or as a paging group. A single interface controller can be presented in code via a call to the *presentControllerWithName* method, passing through as parameters the identifier name of the interface controller to be displayed and an optional object containing context data which will be passed to the modal interface controller via the *awakeWithContext* lifecycle method. For example, the following code fragment modally presents the interface controller with the identifier matching "controllerTwo":

```
presentControllerWithName("controllerTwo", context: contextObj)
```

A set of interface controllers organized using page-based navigation may be presented modally from within code using the *presentControllerWithNames* method passing through arrays containing the controller identifiers and corresponding context objects:

```
presentControllerWithNames(["controllerOne", "controllerTwo"],
        contexts: [contextObj1, contextObj2])
```

By default, the dismissal option displayed in the modal scene will be labelled "Cancel". This can be changed by setting the title property of the interface controller to the desired text.

9.6 **Modal Presentation using Storyboard Segues**

An alternative to writing code to present an interface controller modally involves the use of storyboard segues. All that is required to implement a modal segue is to Ctrl-click on the user interface object within the scene that is to trigger the modal transition and then drag the line to the scene that is to be presented. If a modal segue can be established, the destination scene will highlight as shown in Figure 9-5. If the scene does not highlight, a segue cannot be established. It is not possible, for example, to establish a segue from a Label object because labels, unlike Button objects, do not trigger an event when tapped by the user.

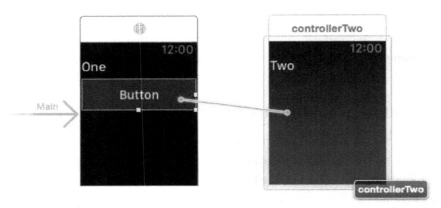

Figure 9-5

Upon release of the line, the segue menu will appear from which the *modal* option should be selected:

Figure 9-6

To modally present a collection of interface controllers grouped together using page-based navigation, simply connect the scenes together within the storyboard using *next page* segues as previously described.

9.7 Passing Context Data During a Modal Segue

The segue connection illustrated in Figure 9-5 above will cause the second interface controller to be presented modally when the button in the first interface controller is tapped by the user. If that is the only functionality that is required then no further steps are necessary when working with modal segues. If, on the other hand, context data needs to be passed during the segue transition then an additional step is needed.

When working with segues, the context data to be passed to the destination interface controllers can be specified by overriding either the *contextForSegueWithIdentifier* or *contextsForSegueWithIdentifier* method within the interface controller from which the segue is originating. The *contextForSegueWithIdentifier* method can be used to pass context data when presenting a single modal interface controller while the *contextsForSegueWithIdentifier* method is used when passing multiple context objects during the transition to a page-based set of interface controllers. In each case, the method will be called by the WatchKit framework during the scene transition and must return either a single context object, or in the case of the *contextsForSegueWithIdentifier* method, an array of context objects. The following code listing shows an example implementation of the method configured to return a string as the context object:

```
override func contextForSegueWithIdentifier(segueIdentifier: String)
     -> AnyObject? {
   return("MyContextString")
}
```

The context objects returned by these methods are passed to the corresponding destination interface controllers via the *awakeWithContext* lifecycle method.

9.8 **Summary**

Page-based navigation within WatchKit apps allows a sequence of interface controller scenes to be navigated by the user through left and right swiping motions performed on the display of the Apple Watch device. The interface controllers that comprise a page-based collection are grouped together within a storyboard file through the implementation of *next page* segues between each controller. Page-based interface controller groups may also be managed at runtime using the *reloadRootControllersWithNames* and *becomeCurrentPage* methods.

Interface controllers may be presented modally either by setting up a modal segue within a storyboard file, or from within code via method calls. The destination of a modal transition can take the form of either a single interface controller or a group of page-based controllers. Each modal controller displays an option for the user to return to the originating interface controller. Mechanisms are also provided for passing context data to the modal interface controller from the originating controller.

Chapter 10

Chapter 10

10. A WatchKit Page-based Interface Tutorial

This chapter will work through the creation of an example that makes use of both page-based navigation and modal interface controller presentation within a WatchKit app.

The project created in this chapter will involve a variation on the fitness app created in the chapter entitled *A WatchKit Table Tutorial*. In this case, the user interface will consist of a sequence of scenes within a page-based interface, each containing a fitness exercise image and a button. When selected by the user, the button will cause a modal interface controller to appear containing a Timer object which will show the user how much time is left to perform the corresponding workout step. When the countdown reaches zero, the app extension will use the taptic engine within the Apple Watch device to physically notify the user via haptic feedback that the time has elapsed.

10.1 Creating the Page Example Project

Start Xcode and create a new iOS project. On the template screen choose the *Application* option located under *watchOS* in the left hand panel and select *iOS App with WatchKit App*. Click *Next*, set the product name to *PageDemoApp*, enter your organization identifier and make sure that the *Devices* menu is set to *Universal*. Before clicking *Next*, change the *Language* menu to Swift and make sure that the *Include* options are all switched off. On the final screen, choose a location in which to store the project files and click on *Create* to proceed to the main Xcode project window.

10.2 Adding the Image Files to the Project

Before designing the interface controller scene, some image files need to be added to the project. These are contained within the *fitness_icons_large* folder of the sample code download which may be obtained from the following URL:

http://www.ebookfrenzy.com/print/watchos2/index.php

Within the Project Navigator panel, select the *Assets.xcassets* entry listed under the *PageDemoApp WatchKit App* folder so that the asset catalog panel appears. Ctrl-click in the left hand panel of the asset catalog and select the *Import...* option from the resulting menu.

In the file import selection panel, navigate to and select the *fitness_icons_large* folder before clicking on the *Open* button. The images will be imported into the asset catalog as an image set named *fitness_icons_large*.

10.3 Designing the First Interface Controller Scene

The user interface for the app is going to consist of three scenes, each containing an Image object and a Button. Select the *Interface.storyboard* file located under *PageDemoApp WatchKit App* in the Project Navigator panel, locate the main scene in the Interface Builder tool and add an Image and a Button object to the scene so that it appears as shown in Figure 10-1:

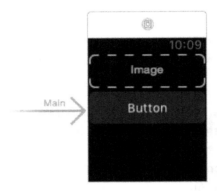

Figure 10-1

Select the Image object in the scene, display the Attributes Inspector and select the *walking* image from the *Image* menu. With the image object still selected and remaining in the Attributes Inspector, change the *Mode* setting to *Aspect Fit* and the *Horizontal* alignment attribute to *Center*.

Double click on the Button object and change the text so it reads "Start". Keep the Button object selected and change the *Vertical* Alignment property in the Attributes Inspector to *Bottom*. On completion of these settings the layout should match that shown in Figure 10-2:

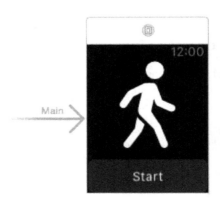

Figure 10-2

10.4 **Adding More Interface Controllers**

This phase of the project requires that an additional two interface controllers be added to the storyboard file. Locate the Interface Controller item in the Object Library panel and drag and drop two instances onto the storyboard canvas so that the objects are positioned to the right of the main controller (Figure 10-3):

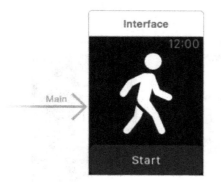

Figure 10-3

Since the user interface design for the remaining two scenes will be similar to that of the first, a quicker option than manually designing the scenes is to cut and paste the objects from the first scene. Hold down the Shift key and click on the Image and Button objects in the main scene. Press Cmd-C to copy the objects, select the second interface controller scene and use Cmd-V to paste the objects into the scene. Select the third scene and perform the paste operation once again.

Select the Image object in the second scene, display the Attributes Inspector and change the image value to the *treadmill* image. Repeat this step to change the image in the third scene to *weights*. On completion of these steps, the three interface controller scenes should appear as shown in Figure 10-4:

Figure 10-4

10.5 **Establishing the Segues**

For the three interface controllers to work within a page-based navigation interface, the controllers must be connected using *next page* segues. To achieve this, Ctrl-click on the title bar of the first scene (the title bar is the area which currently shows the time). Drag the resulting line to the second interface controller until it highlights (Figure 10-5) and release the line. In the segue relationship menu select the *next page* option.

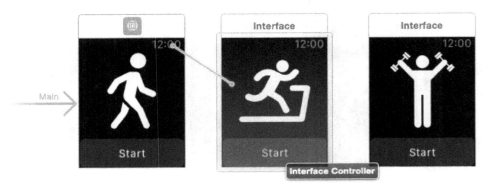

Figure 10-5

Repeat the above steps to establish a segue between the second and third interface controllers so that the storyboard matches that of Figure 10-6:

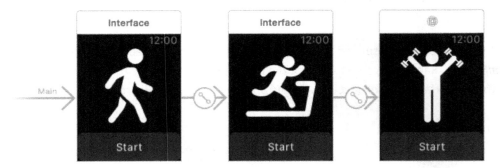

Figure 10-6

Run the app and test that the three scenes can now be navigated by making swiping motions on the display:

Figure 10-7

10.6 Assigning Interface Controllers

The scene now consists of three scenes but at the moment only the first scene has an Interface Controller associated with it. One approach to take at this point might be to add two new interface controller classes to the project, one for each of the two remaining scenes in the page-based navigation set. Since all three scenes essentially perform the same task, however, a more efficient approach is to use the same interface controller class for all three. The first scene is already assigned to the InterfaceController class, so select the second scene so that it is highlighted in blue, display the Identity Inspector panel and change the *Class* menu setting to *InterfaceController* (Figure 10-8). Repeat these steps with the third interface controller selected.

Figure 10-8

In each case, make sure that the *Module* menu is set to *PageDemoApp_WatchKit_Extension*.

10.7 Adding the Timer Interface Controller

When the Start button is tapped on any of the paged controller scenes an additional scene will be modally displayed to the user. This scene will contain a single object in the form of a WKInterfaceTimer instance. Start by dragging and dropping an Interface Controller object from the Object Library panel so that it is positioned beneath the three existing scenes in the storyboard:

Figure 10-9

Drag and drop a Timer object from the Object Library onto the newly added scene. With the Timer object selected, display the Attributes Inspector panel and set the *Horizontal* and *Vertical* alignment attributes to *Center*.

Click on the "T" button within the Font text field, select *System* from the popup panel, *Bold* from the *Style* menu and set the *Size* setting to 28 as shown in Figure 10-10:

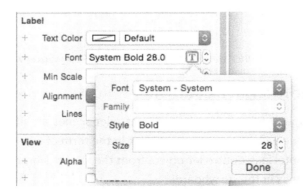

Figure 10-10

On completion of these steps the scene should match that illustrated in Figure 10-11:

Figure 10-11

By default, the Timer object displays hours, minutes and seconds as numbers (referred to as *positional* format). A range of other configuration alternatives is available within the Attributes Inspector for changing both what is displayed on the timer and how it is displayed. It is, for example, possible to also display month, week, day and year values. It is also possible to change the way in which this information is displayed, including fully spelling out the time and date in words instead of numbers. Although this example will use the default setting, it is worth reviewing the options in the Attributes Inspector panel for future reference.

Locate and select the *PageDemoApp WatchKit Extension* entry in the Xcode Project Navigator panel, Ctrl-click on it and select the *New File…* menu option. Create a new watchOS WatchKit Class file named *TimerInterfaceController* subclassed from *WKInterfaceController* and proceed with the steps to generate the class source file into the *PageDemoApp WatchKit Extension* project folder.

Return to the *Interface.storyboard* file, select the timer scene so that it is highlighted in blue and, using the Identity Inspector panel, change the *Class* menu to *TimerInterfaceController*. Switch to the Attributes Inspector panel and enter *TimerInterfaceController* into the *Identifier* field.

Select the Timer object in the timer scene, display the Assistant Editor panel and verify that it is displaying the source code for the *TimerInterfaceController.swift* file. Ctrl-click on the Timer object and drag the resulting line to a position immediately after the class declaration line in the Assistant Editor panel. Release the line and establish an outlet named *workoutTimer*. On completion of these steps the start of the *TimerInterfaceController.swift* file should read as follows:

```
import WatchKit
import Foundation

class TimerInterfaceController: WKInterfaceController {
```

```
@IBOutlet weak var workoutTimer: WKInterfaceTimer!

override func awakeWithContext(context: AnyObject?) {
    super.awakeWithContext(context)

    // Configure interface objects here.
}
    .
    .
    .
}
```

With the timer interface controller added and configured, the next step is to implement the modal segues so that the interface controller is presented when the Start buttons are tapped.

10.8 Adding the Modal Segues

When the buttons on the three paged scenes are tapped by the user, the timer scene will need to be displayed modally. Establish the first segue by Ctrl-clicking on the Button object in the first scene and dragging to the timer scene. Release the line and select the *modal* option from the Action Segue menu. Repeat these steps for the Button objects on the remaining two scenes so that the storyboard resembles Figure 10-12:

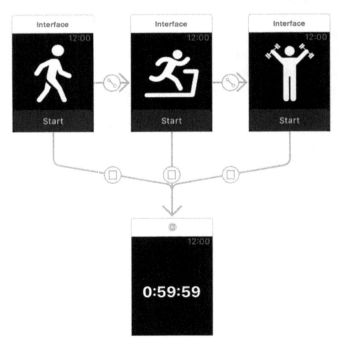

Figure 10-12

Compile and run the app and verify that tapping the button on each of the scenes causes the scene for the timer interface controller to appear. Note that a Cancel option is provided on the timer scene to return to the original scene.

10.9 **Configuring the Context Data**

When the timer interface controller is presented it will need to be initialized with a countdown time. The amount of time will vary depending on the scene from which the timer was launched. This means that we will need to find a way to identify which of the three modal segues triggered the appearance of the timer interface controller and, based on that information, pass the appropriate time duration through as context data.

The first step in this process is to establish a way to distinguish one segue from another by assigning identifiers. Begin by selecting the segue line from the left most scene to the timer scene and displaying the Attributes Inspector panel. Within the panel, enter *walkSegue* into the *Identifier* field as shown in Figure 10-13:

Figure 10-13

Follow the same steps to assign identifiers to the two remaining modal segues named *runSegue* and *weightsSegue* respectively. To avoid encountering a known problem with Xcode whereby the identifiers are not saved, be sure to save the storyboard after entering identifier (Cmd-S).

As explained in the chapter entitled *WatchKit Page Based User Interfaces and Modal Interface Controllers*, context data can be passed during a modal segue transition by implementing the *contextForSegueWithIdentifier* method within the originating interface controller. Passed as a parameter to this method is the identifier of the segue that triggered the call, allowing us to configure the context data according to the segue.

Select the *InterfaceController.swift* file and implement the *contextForSegueWithIdentifier* method so that it reads as follows:

```
override func contextForSegueWithIdentifier(segueIdentifier: String) ->
AnyObject? {

    var contextValue: NSTimeInterval?
```

```
        switch (segueIdentifier) {
            case "walkSegue":
                contextValue = 10
            case "runSegue":
                contextValue = 20
            case "weightsSegue":
                contextValue = 30
            default:
                break
        }
        return(contextValue)
    }
```

The code in the above method declares a variable in which to store the countdown time before using a switch construct to identify the current segue and select a time value which is then returned. The duration value will then be passed by the WatchKit framework to the destination interface controller via the *awakeWithContext* method of that class. For testing purposes, the duration values are set to seconds rather than minutes.

10.10 Configuring the Timer

When the timer interface controller is now displayed it will be passed a time duration value via the *awakeWithContext* lifecycle method. This time duration will subsequently need to be assigned to the Timer object in the scene and the countdown started. The WatchKit Timer object is initialized by passing through an NSDate object configured to the current time, a time in the future or a time in the past. Passing through the current time and date will cause the timer to begin counting upwards from 0:00. Passing through a date and time in the future will cause the timer to begin counting down towards that time and date. Specifying a date and time in the past, on the other hand, will start the timer at that date and time and begin counting upwards from that point.

Select the *TimerInterfaceController.swift* file, locate the *awakeWithContext* method and modify it so that it reads as follows:

```
override func awakeWithContext(context: AnyObject?) {
    super.awakeWithContext(context)

    if let duration: AnyObject = context {
        let date = NSDate(timeIntervalSinceNow:
                            duration as! NSTimeInterval)
        workoutTimer.setDate(date)
        workoutTimer.start()
    }
}
```

The code verifies that a time value was passed through as the context object and uses that value to create an NSDate object configured to a time point in the future. The configured NSDate object is then used to initialize the Timer object using the previously configured outlet before the countdown is started.

Run the application and note that the timer is now initialized and begins counting down when the timer scene is presented. The time duration should also differ depending on which scene triggers the segue as defined in the earlier switch statement:

Figure 10-14

10.11 Playing the Haptic Effect

The final feature to be added to the project is to set up to notify the user that the timer has reached zero. The problem that arises in implementing this behavior is that the WatchKit Timer object does not trigger an action when it reaches zero. The solution is to initialize an NSTimer instance to run for the same amount of time as the WatchKit Timer object and configured to call a selector method when the time has elapsed. The code to set up the NSTimer object needs to be added to the *awakeWithContext* method as follows:

```
override func awakeWithContext(context: AnyObject?) {
    super.awakeWithContext(context)

    if let duration: AnyObject = context {

        NSTimer.scheduledTimerWithTimeInterval(
                duration as! NSTimeInterval,
                target: self,
                selector: Selector("playAlert"),
                userInfo: nil,
                repeats: false)
```

```
        let date = NSDate(timeIntervalSinceNow:
                    duration as NSTimeInterval)
        workoutTimer.setDate(date)
        workoutTimer.start()
    }
}
```

The NSTimer object is configured to call a selector method named *playAlert* when the designated time has elapsed. The code in this method simply needs to obtain a reference to the current WKInterfaceDevice object and call the *playHaptic* method on that object, passing through a request for the Notification style of alert.

Edit the *TimerInterfaceController.swift* file and implement the *playAlert* method as follows:

```
func playAlert() {
    let device = WKInterfaceDevice.currentDevice()
    device.playHaptic(.Notification)
}
```

With the haptic feedback added to the project, compile and run the app on an Apple Watch device and test that the watch triggers a haptic "nudge" and plays the notification sound when the countdown reaches zero in the timer interface controller scene.

10.12 Summary

This chapter has worked through the design and implementation of an example WatchKit app containing a page-based scene navigation interface. The example also highlighted the steps involved in implementing modal interface controller presentation and the passing of context during segue transitions. The chapter also introduced the WatchKit Timer object and explored the use of an NSTimer instance in parallel with a Timer object to receive notification of the timer reaching zero.

11. Handling User Input in a WatchKit App

U nlike the iPhone, the Apple Watch display is too small to accommodate a virtual keyboard to allow the user to input text into an app. This does not, however, mean that it is not possible to accept user input. In fact, the WatchKit framework provides a mechanism for user input in the form of selections from a list of phrases, voice dictation and emoji image selection.

This chapter will provide an overview of how to accept user input from within a WatchKit app before providing a brief tutorial.

11.1 Getting User Input

The WatchKit framework supports three types of user input in the form of phrase selection, voice dictation and emoji image selection. All three forms of input are available via a single modal scene, an example of which is illustrated in Figure 11-1:

Figure 11-1

This screen is referred to as the *text input controller* and can be configured with a list of phrases to be displayed, to enable or disable support for emoji selection, or to go directly to dictation input.

11.2 **Displaying the Text Input Controller**

The text input controller screen is displayed via a call to the *presentTextInputControllerWithSuggestions* method of the currently active interface controller instance. The method accepts as parameters an array of phrase suggestion strings and an input mode value indicating what forms of input are to be accepted. The method also requires a completion handler block to be called when the input session is completed. This completion block is passed an array containing the results of the input.

The following code, for example, invokes the text input controller with emoji support and a range of phrase suggestions. The completion handler block simply outputs the input string from the reply array to the console:

```
let phrases = ["I'm in a meeting", "I'll call you later", "Call me later"]

presentTextInputControllerWithSuggestions(phrases,
                     allowedInputMode: .AllowEmoji,
                     completion: { (result) -> Void in

    if let choice = result {
            print(choice[0])
    }
})
```

The above code used the *.AllowEmoji* option (or more precisely the *WKTextInputMode.AllowEmoji* option) to include static emoji images as selection options. The three input mode options supported by WatchKit are as follows:

- **WKTextInputMode.Plain** – Allows the user to generate input from the phrase selection list and dictation only. The emoji button is absent from the text input controller screen in this mode.
- **WKTextInputMode.AllowEmoji** - Allows the user to generate input using the phrase list, dictation and non-animated emoji images.
- **WKTextInputMode.AllowAnimatedEmoji** - Allows the user to generate input using the phrase list, dictation and both animated and non-animated emoji images.

The text input controller screen will automatically dismiss when the user has made an input selection or tapped the Cancel button. The controller may also be dismissed from within the code of the interface controller via a call to the *dismissTextInputController* method. When the text input controller is dismissed in this way, the code within the completion handler block is not executed.

When testing text input, it is important to note that emoji and dictation modes are not available from within the simulator environment.

11.3 **Detecting if Input is a String or NSData Object**

If the input is in the form of text or a non-animated emoji, the input will be returned in the form of a Unicode string contained within a String object. If the user selects an animated emoji, however, the image will be returned in the form of an NSData object. The following code can be used to identify whether the returned result is a String or NSData object:

```
if let choice = result {
    if choice[0] is String {
        // Result is a String object
        // Handle as a text string
    }

    if choice[0] is NSData {
        // Result is an NSData object
        // Handle as an image
    }
}
```

11.4 **Direct Dictation Input**

In many situations, input will be needed only through the use of dictation. To move directly to dictation based input, call the *presentTextInputControllerWithSuggestions* method without any suggested phrases and with the input mode set to *.Plain*. For example:

```
presentTextInputControllerWithSuggestions(nil,
            allowedInputMode: .Plain,
            completion: { (result) -> Void in


    }
})
```

11.5 **Creating the User Input Example Project**

Start Xcode and create a new iOS project. On the template screen choose the *Application* option located under *watchOS* in the left hand panel and select *iOS App with WatchKit App*. Click *Next,* set the product name to *TextInputApp,* enter your organization identifier and make sure that the *Devices* menu is set to *Universal*. Before clicking *Next*, change the *Language* menu to Swift and verify that all of the *Include* options are switched off. On the final screen, choose a location in which to store the project files and click on *Create* to proceed to the main Xcode project window.

11.6 **Designing the WatchKit App Main Scene**

Locate and select the *Interface.storyboard* file so that it loads into Interface Builder. Drag and drop a Button object from the Object Library panel, double-click on it and change the text so that it reads "Get Input".

Add a Label object to the scene and set both the *Horizontal* and *Vertical* alignment properties in the Attributes Inspector panel to *Center* so that the scene layout matches that of Figure 11-2. Also, increase the *Lines* property to 4 so that multiple lines of text input can be displayed if necessary:

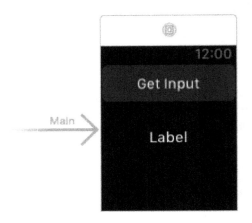

Figure 11-2

Display the Assistant Editor, Ctrl-click on the Label object in the storyboard scene and drag the resulting line to a position immediately beneath the class declaration line in the Assistant Editor panel. On releasing the line, establish an outlet named *labelObject* in the connection panel.

Repeat these steps on the Button object, this time establishing an action connection to a method named *getUserInput*.

11.7 **Getting the User Input**

The code to get input from the user now needs to be implemented within the *getUserInput* action method. For the purposes of this example, input will be accepted in the form of dictation, non-animated emoji and via phrase list selection. Once obtained, the user input will be displayed on the Label object within the main scene. Locate and select the *InterfaceController.swift* file for the WatchKit app extension in the Project Navigator panel and modify the *getUserInput* method so that it reads as follows:

```
@IBAction func getUserInput() {
    let phrases = ["I'm in a meeting", "I'll call you later", "Call me
later"]
```

```
presentTextInputControllerWithSuggestions(phrases,
        allowedInputMode: .AllowEmoji,
        completion: { (result) -> Void in

    if let choice = result {
        self.labelObject.setText(choice[0] as? String)
    }
})
}
```

11.8 Testing the Application

Compile and run the WatchKit app on a physical Apple Watch device, tap on the *Get Input* button and use dictation to enter some text. On tapping the Done button the dictated text will appear on the Label object in the main scene of the app. Repeat these steps to test the phrase selection and emoji forms of input.

11.9 Summary

WatchKit provides support for user input via phrase selection, dictation and emoji images. Input is initiated using the *presentTextInputControllerWithSuggestions* method of the currently active interface controller instance. This chapter has covered the basics of user input in WatchKit and worked through the creation of an example WatchKit app project.

12. An Introduction to Watch Connectivity in watchOS 2

When watchOS 1 was introduced it provided a minimal level of support for the implementation of communication between an iOS app running on an iPhone and the corresponding WatchKit app running on a paired Apple Watch. The shortcomings of watchOS 1 have been addressed in watchOS 2 with the introduction of the WatchConnectivity framework.

As will be outlined in this chapter, the WatchConnectivity framework provides a range of options for implementing bi-directional communication between WatchKit and iOS apps including the transfer of files and data and the exchange of interactive messages.

12.1 Watch Connectivity Communication Options

Watch Connectivity provides four different ways in which an iOS app and the corresponding WatchKit app can communicate:

12.1.1 Application Context Mode

Application context mode allows small amounts of data contained in a dictionary object to be passed between one app and another. The data is transferred in the background and delivered to the receiving app via a delegate method the next time the receiving app runs. The time at which the background transfer occurs is dependent upon the operating system based on factors such as battery status and device activity.

If more recent data is sent by the sending app before the background transfer has taken place, the older data is overwritten by the new data. This ensures that when the transfer takes place, only the most recent data will be delivered to the receiving app.

12.1.2 User Information Transfer Mode

User information transfer mode is similar to application context mode in that it facilitates the transfer of small amounts of dictionary based data between apps. As with application context mode, transfers are performed in the background subject to timing decided by the system. Unlike application context mode, however, user information transfers are placed in a delivery queue so that each message will be received by the destination app.

12.1.3 File Transfer Mode

As the name suggest, file transfer mode allows files to be transferred between apps. Transfers are performed in the background and placed in a temporary directory on the destination device from which they must be moved to avoid subsequent deletion by the system.

12.1.4 Interactive Messaging Mode

Interactive messaging mode allows messages to be sent immediately to the receiving app. The receiving app is notified of the message arrival via a delegate method call and passed the message. Messages are delivered in the order in which they are sent.

Before sending an interactive message, the sending app must first check that the destination app is *reachable*. For a WatchKit app to be reachable it must be installed and currently running on the Apple Watch device. Since the iOS app is launched automatically in the background when an interactive message arrives, it is considered to be reachable even when not currently running.

Interactive messages provide the option to pass through a reply handler which may subsequently be called by the receiving app and used to return data to the sending app.

Interactive messaging supports the transfer of both Dictionary-based data and NSData objects.

12.2 WatchConnectivity Session Creation

Regardless of the type of communication to be used, a number of session initialization tasks must be performed prior to making any send requests. It only makes sense to perform these steps, however, if the device on which the app is running supports Watch Connectivity (Watch Connectivity is not, for example, supported when an app is running on an iPad).

Whether or not the device on which an app is running supports Watch Connectivity can be identified by calling the *isSupported* method of the WCSession class as follows:

```
import WatchConnectivity
    .
    .
    .
if (WCSession.isSupported()) {
     // Watch Connectivity is supported
}
```

If Watch Connectivity is supported, the next steps are to obtain a reference to the default connectivity session for the app, designate a class instance to act as the session delegate and then activate the session:

```
import WatchConnectivity
```

```
.
.
.
if (WCSession.isSupported()) {
    let session = WCSession.defaultSession()
    session.delegate = self
    session.activateSession()
}
```

It is important to note that the class instance designated as the session delegate must conform to the WCSessionDelegate protocol and that it is the methods within this class that will be called by the system to notify the app of incoming WatchConnectivity content and messages.

A key point of which to be aware is that the above initialization steps must be performed on *both* the iOS and WatchKit app in order for communication to take place.

12.3 Obtaining Session State Information

Once a session is active, a variety of properties can be used within the iOS app to obtain additional information relating to the session. It is possible, for example, to verify that the iPhone is currently paired with an Apple Watch:

```
if session.paired == true {
    // Devices are paired
}
```

It is also possible to check from within the iOS app whether the companion WatchKit app is installed on the paired Apple Watch device:

```
if session.watchAppInstalled == true {
    // WatchKit app is installed
}
```

Two methods may also be implemented within the session delegate class to receive notification of when either the session state or the reachability of an app changes during a communication session:

```
func sessionReachabilityDidChange(session: WCSession) {
    // Handle change in reachability
}

func sessionWatchStateDidChange(session: WCSession) {
    // Handle session state change
}
```

When using interactive messaging mode, it is important to verify that the corresponding app is reachable before attempting to send a message:

```
if session.reachable == true {
    // App is reachable
}
```

When working with clock face complications, it is also possible to verify whether the complication associated with the WatchKit app is installed in the user's clock face by checking the *complicationEnabled* property:

```
if session.complicationEnabled == true {
    // Complication is enabled
}
```

The topic of complications will be covered in greater detail beginning with the chapter entitled *An Overview of ClockKit and Apple Watch Complications*.

12.4 The watchDirectoryURL Property

For as long as the WatchKit app is installed on the Apple Watch and the *watchAppInstalled* session property returns a true value, the *watchDirectoryURL* session property will contain the path to the *watch directory*. This is a container on the watch into which can be stored any data needed by the current installation instance of the WatchKit app such as preferences or files waiting to be transferred. The directory will remain in place until the user removes the WatchKit app from the Apple Watch device at which point the directory and all its content will be deleted from the device.

12.5 Sending and Receiving Application Context Data

Once the Watch Connectivity session has been established by both the iOS and WatchKit apps, application context data may be packaged into a dictionary object and transferred via a call to the *updateApplicationContext* method of the default session as demonstrated in the following code fragment:

```
do {
    let session = WCSession.defaultSession()
    let context = ["FlightTime" : "Delayed"]
    try session.updateApplicationContext(context)

} catch let error as NSError {
    print("Error: \(error.description)")
}
```

The receiving app will be notified of the arrival of a context update via a call to the *session:didReceiveApplicationContext* method of the object designated as the delegate during the session initialization process. If the destination app is already running, the method will be called as soon as the transfer is complete. In the event that the app is not running when the context data is transferred, the method will be called next time the app is launched by the user. Passed through as a parameter to this method is the dictionary object containing the context data:

```
func session(session: WCSession, didReceiveApplicationContext
applicationContext: [String : AnyObject]) {
    print("Received context")
    print(applicationContext["FlightTime"])
}
```

12.6 Sending and Receiving User Information Data

User information data is transferred using the *transferUserInfo* method of the default session instance as follows:

```
let session = WCSession.defaultSession()
let userInfo = ["NewMessage" : msgTitle]
session.transferUserInfo(userInfo)
```

The receiving app will be notified of the arrival of user info data via a call to the *session:didReceiveUserInfo* method of the object designated as the delegate during the session initialization process. If the destination app is already running, the method will be called as soon as the transfer is complete. In the event that the app is not running when the context data is transferred the method will be called next time the app is launched by the user. Passed through as a parameter to this method is the dictionary object containing the user info data. If multiple user info transfers are pending the method is called once for each delivery:

```
func session(session: WCSession, didReceiveUserInfo userInfo: [String :
AnyObject]) {
    print("Received user info")
    print(userInfo["NewMessage"])
}
```

As previously outlined, multiple user info transfers are placed in a queue ready for transfer and then transmitted at a time decided by the system. Details of any transfers that have yet to be completed may be obtained at any time from within the sending app via a call to the *outstandingUserInfoTransfers* session method as follows:

```
let pending = session.outstandingUserInfoTransfers()
```

A list of pending transfers is returned in the form of an array of WCUserInfoTransfer objects containing the data being transferred and a Boolean value indicating whether the transfer is currently in progress. A call to the *cancel* method of an object will remove that object from the transfer queue.

12.7 **Transferring Files**

Files are transferred using the *transferFile* method of the default session and are placed in a queue until the transfer is completed in the background. The *transferFile* method takes as parameters the URL of the file to be transferred together with an optional dictionary containing metadata. The following code, for example, initiates the transfer of an image file:

```
let session = WCSession.defaultSession()
let url = NSBundle.mainBundle().URLForResource("myimage",
            withExtension: "png")

session.transferFile(url!, metadata: nil)
```

As with user info data mode, if more than one transfer is initiated the transfers are queued by the system. Once a transfer is complete the *session:didReceiveFile* method of the session delegate is called and passed a WCSessionFile object containing the URL and metadata for the file. If the app is not running when the transfer completes the method is called the next time the app is launched.

The transferred file is placed in the *Document/Inbox* folder of the destination app and will be deleted once the delegate method returns. As such it is essential that the transferred file be moved to a permanent location as soon as the destination app receives notification of transfer completion. The following sample implementation of the *session:didReceiveFile* delegate method moves the transferred file to the Document directory:

```
func session(session: WCSession, didReceiveFile file: WCSessionFile) {

    let dirPaths = NSSearchPathForDirectoriesInDomains(.DocumentDirectory,
                .UserDomainMask, true)
    let docsDir = dirPaths[0] as String
    let filemgr = NSFileManager.defaultManager()

    do {
        try filemgr.moveItemAtPath(file.fileURL.path!,
            toPath: docsDir + "/myimage.png")
    } catch let error as NSError {
        print("Error moving file: \(error.description)")
    }
}
```

An array of WCSessionFileTransfer file transfer objects that have yet to be completed may be obtained at any time from within the sending app via a call to the *outstandingUserInfoTransfers* session method as follows:

```
let pending = session.outstandingFileTransfers()
```

The information available within each WCSessionFileTransfer object in the array includes access to the file awaiting transfer and a property indicating whether or not the transfer is currently in progress. A call to the *cancel* method of such an object will end the transfer and remove the file from the transfer queue.

12.8 Sending and Receiving Interactive Messages

Interactive messages can take the form of a dictionary object using the *sendMessage* method, or an NSData object using the *SendMessageData* method. In addition to the message content, these methods may also be passed an optional replyHandler reference. This takes the form of a closure containing the code to be called by the receiving app providing a convenient mechanism by which data can be returned to the sending app. The option is also available to pass through an error handler which can be used by the receiving app to return error information. Before attempting to send a message from the iOS app to the WatchKit app, the code should always first check that the destination app is reachable.

The following code demonstrates the use of the *sendMessage* method, in this case passing through both reply and error handlers:

```
if WCSession.defaultSession().reachable == true {

    let requestValues = ["command" : "start"]

    let session = WCSession.defaultSession()

    session.sendMessage(requestValues, replyHandler: { reply in

        // Code to handle reply here

    }, errorHandler: { error in

        // Code to handle error here

    })
}
```

When a message is received, either the *session:didReceiveMessage* method or the *session:didReceiveMessageData* method of the session delegate will be called. It is important to note that there are two forms of these methods, one which expects a reply handler and one which does not. Be sure to implement the correct one within the session delegate depending on whether or not the sent message includes a reply handler. The following example method implementation expects the received message to contain a reply handler reference which it subsequently calls to return data to the sending app:

```
func session(session: WCSession, didReceiveMessage message: [String :
AnyObject], replyHandler: ([String : AnyObject]) -> Void) {

    var replyValues = ["status" : "playing"] // Data to be returned


    // Code to process message here

    replyHandler(replyValues) // Return data to sending app
}
```

12.9 Summary

Watch Connectivity is a new framework included with the watchOS 2 SDK designed to enable bi-directional communication between an iOS app and the corresponding WatchKit app. Watch Connectivity supports the background transfer of data and files back and forth between the two apps and also the implementation of interactive messaging between apps.

Having provided an overview of Watch Connectivity, the next chapter (entitled *A WatchConnectivity Messaging Tutorial*) will provide a practical example of the use of interactive messaging.

13. A WatchConnectivity Messaging Tutorial

The previous chapter explored the use of the different forms of communication provided by the WatchConnectivity framework to enable a WatchKit app to communicate with the corresponding iOS app. The tutorial outlined in this chapter will make use of the interactive messaging Watch Connectivity feature to control the playback of audio on the iPhone device from a WatchKit app running on a paired Apple Watch.

13.1 About the Project

The project created in this chapter will consist of two parts. The first is an iOS application that allows the user to playback music and to adjust the volume level from an iPhone device. The second part of the project involves a WatchKit app designed to allow the user the same level of control over the audio playback on the iPhone from the paired Apple Watch device. The communication back and forth between the WatchKit and iOS apps will be implemented entirely using the interactive messaging feature of the WatchConnectivity framework.

13.2 Creating the Project

Start Xcode and create a new iOS project. On the template screen choose the *Application* option located under *watchOS* in the left hand panel and select *iOS App with WatchKit App* from the main panel. Click *Next,* set the product name to *WatchConnectApp,* enter your organization identifier and make sure that the *Devices* menu is set to *Universal*. Before clicking *Next*, change the *Language* menu to Swift and turn off each of the *Include* options. On the final screen, choose a location in which to store the project files and click on *Create* to proceed to the main Xcode project window.

13.3 Enabling Audio Background Mode

When the user begins audio playback it should not stop until either the user taps the stop button or the end of the audio track is reached. To ensure that the iOS app is not suspended by the operating system the Audio background mode needs to be enabled. Within Xcode, select the *WatchConnectApp* target at the top of the Project Navigator panel, select the Capabilities tab and switch the Background Modes option from *Off* to *On*. Once background modes are enabled, enable the checkbox next to *Audio, Airplay and Picture in Picture* as outlined in Figure 13-1:

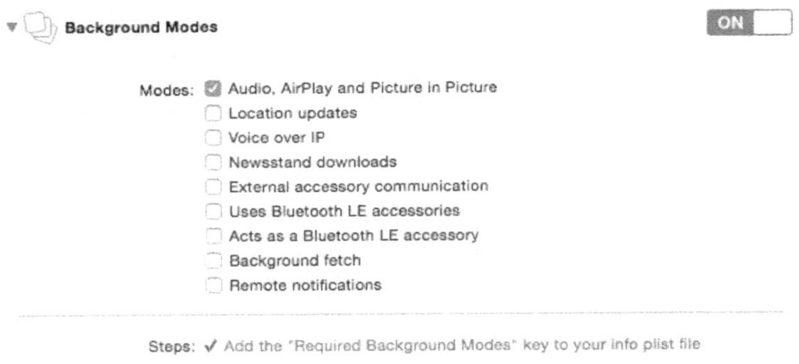

Figure 13-1

With this mode enabled, the background iOS app will not be suspended as long as it continues to play audio. It will also allow the iOS app to be launched in the background and begin audio playback at the request of the WatchKit app.

13.4 Designing the iOS App User Interface

The user interface for the iOS app will consist of a Play button, a Stop button and a slider with which to control the volume level. Locate and select the *Main.storyboard* file in the Xcode Project Navigator panel and drag and drop two Buttons and one Slider view onto the scene canvas so that they are centered horizontally within the scene. Double click on each button, changing the text to "Play" and "Stop" respectively, and stretch the slider so that it is slightly wider than the default width. On completion of these steps the layout should resemble that of Figure 13-2:

Figure 13-2

Using the *Resolve Auto Layout Issues* menu (indicated in Figure 13-3) select the *Reset to Suggested Constraints* option to configure appropriate layout behavior for the three views in the scene:

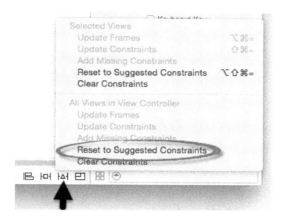

Figure 13-3

13.5 Establishing Outlets and Actions

With the *Main.storyboard* file still loaded into Interface Builder, display the Assistant Editor panel and verify that it is displaying the content of the *ViewController.swift* file. Ctrl-click on the Slider object in the storyboard scene and drag the resulting line to a position immediately beneath the class declaration line in the Assistant Editor panel. On releasing the line, establish an outlet named *volumeControl* in the connection panel.

Repeat these steps on both of the Button views, this time establishing action connections to methods named *playAudio* and *stopAudio* respectively.

Finally, establish an action connection for the Slider view to a method named *sliderMoved* based on the *Value Changed* event. On completion of these steps the *ViewController.swift* file should read as follows:

```
import UIKit

class ViewController: UIViewController {

    @IBOutlet weak var volumeControl: UISlider!

    override func viewDidLoad() {
        super.viewDidLoad()
        // Do any additional setup after loading the view, typically from a
 nib.
    }

    @IBAction func playAudio(sender: AnyObject) {
```

```
    }

    @IBAction func stopAudio(sender: AnyObject) {
    }

    @IBAction func sliderMoved(sender: AnyObject) {
    }

    override func didReceiveMemoryWarning() {
        super.didReceiveMemoryWarning()
        // Dispose of any resources that can be recreated.
    }
}
```

13.6 Initializing Audio Playback

Before sounds can be played within the iOS app a number of steps need to be taken. First, an audio file needs to be added to the project. The music to be played in this tutorial is contained in a file named *vivaldi.mp3* located in the *audio_files* folder of the sample code download available from the following URL:

http://www.ebookfrenzy.com/print/watchos2/index.php

Locate the file in a Finder window and drag and drop it beneath the *WatchConnectApp* folder in the Project Navigator panel as shown in Figure 13-4, clicking on the *Finish* button in the options panel:

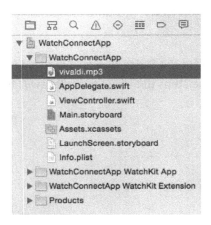

Figure 13-4

With the audio file added to the project, code now needs to be added to the *viewDidLoad* method of the *ViewController.swift* file to initialize an AVAudioPlayer instance so that playback is ready to start when the user taps the Play button. Select the *ViewController.swift* file and modify it to import the AVFoundation framework, declare AVAudioSession and AVAudioPlayer instance variables and to initialize the player:

```swift
import UIKit
import AVFoundation
import MediaPlayer

class ViewController: UIViewController {

    var audioSession: AVAudioSession = AVAudioSession.sharedInstance()
    var audioPlayer: AVAudioPlayer?

    @IBOutlet weak var volumeControl: UISlider!

    override func viewDidLoad() {
        super.viewDidLoad()

        var url: NSURL?

        do {
            try audioSession.setCategory(AVAudioSessionCategoryPlayback)
            url = NSURL.fileURLWithPath(
                NSBundle.mainBundle().pathForResource("vivaldi",
                    ofType: "mp3")!)
        } catch {
            print("AudioSession error")
        }

        do {
            try audioPlayer = AVAudioPlayer(contentsOfURL: url!,
                                fileTypeHint: nil)
            audioPlayer?.prepareToPlay()
            audioPlayer?.volume = 0.1
        } catch let error as NSError {
            print("Error: \(error.description)")
        }
    }
    .
    .
}
```

The code configures the audio session to allow audio playback to be initiated from the background even when the device is locked and the ring switch on the side of the device is set to silent mode. The audio player instance is then configured with the mp3 file containing the audio to be played and an initial volume level set.

13.7 **Implementing the Audio Control Methods**

With the audio player configured and initialized, the next step is to add some methods to control the playback of the music. Remaining within the *ViewController.swift* file, implement these three methods as follows:

```
func stopPlay() {
    audioPlayer?.stop()
}

func startPlay() {
    audioPlayer?.play()
}

func adjustVolume(level: Float)
{
    audioPlayer?.volume = level
}
```

Each of these methods will need to be called by the corresponding action methods:

```
@IBAction func playAudio(sender: AnyObject) {
    startPlay()
}

@IBAction func stopAudio(sender: AnyObject) {
    stopPlay()
}

@IBAction func sliderMoved(sender: AnyObject) {
    adjustVolume(volumeControl.value)
}
```

Compile and run the iOS app and test that the user interface controls allow playback to be started and stopped via the two buttons and that the slider provides control over the volume level.

With the iOS app now functioning, it is time to initialize the WatchConnectivity session for the iOS app.

13.8 **Initializing the iOS App Watch Connectivity Session**

The Watch Connectivity session needs to be initialized as early as possible in the app lifecycle. This process involves checking that the Apple Watch is paired and that the corresponding WatchKit app is installed on the watch device. For the purposes of this example, the code to perform these tasks will be added to the *didFinishLaunchingWithOptions* method located in the *AppDelegate.swift* file as follows, making sure to import the WatchConnectivity framework and to declare the class as implementing the WCSessionDelegate protocol:

```
import UIKit
import WatchConnectivity

@UIApplicationMain
class AppDelegate: UIResponder, UIApplicationDelegate, WCSessionDelegate {

    var window: UIWindow?

    func application(application: UIApplication,
didFinishLaunchingWithOptions launchOptions: [NSObject: AnyObject]?) -> Bool
{

        if (WCSession.isSupported()) {
            let session = WCSession.defaultSession()
            session.delegate = self
            session.activateSession()

            if session.paired != true {
                print("Apple Watch is not paired")
            }

            if session.watchAppInstalled != true {
                print("WatchKit app is not installed")
            }
        } else {
            print("WatchConnectivity is not supported on this device")
        }

        return true
    }
```

13.9 Designing the WatchKit App Scene

Select the *Interface.storyboard* file located under *WatchConnectApp WatchKit App* so that the storyboard loads into Interface Builder. Drag and drop a Label, two Buttons and a Slider from the Object Library onto the scene canvas so that the layout matches that shown in Figure 13-5:

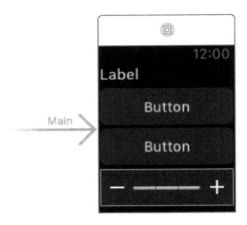

Figure 13-5

Select the Label object, display the Attributes Inspector panel and set the *Alignment* property in the Label section of the panel to center the displayed text. Within the Alignment section of the panel, change the *Horizontal* menu to *Center*.

Double click on the uppermost of the two buttons and change the text to "Play". Repeat this step for the second button, this time changing the text so that it reads "Stop".

Select the Slider object and, in the Attributes Inspector panel, change both the *Maximum* and *Steps* properties to 10.

On completion of the above steps, the scene layout should resemble Figure 13-6:

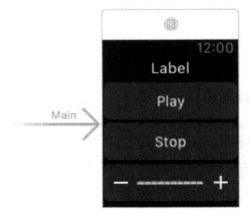

Figure 13-6

Display the Assistant Editor and verify that it is showing the contents of the *InterfaceController.swift* file. Using the Assistant Editor, establish an outlet connection from the Label object in the user interface named *statusLabel.* Next, create action connections from the two buttons named *startPlay* and *stopPlay* respectively and an action connection from the slider named *volumeChange*. With these connections established, the top section of the *InterfaceController.swift* file should read as follows:

```swift
import WatchKit
import Foundation

class InterfaceController: WKInterfaceController {

    @IBOutlet weak var statusLabel: WKInterfaceLabel!

    override func awakeWithContext(context: AnyObject?) {
        super.awakeWithContext(context)

        // Configure interface objects here.
    }

    @IBAction func startPlay() {
    }

    @IBAction func stopPlay() {
    }

    @IBAction func volumeChange(value: Float) {
    }
.
.
}
```

13.10 Initializing the WatchKit App Connectivity Session

Having initialized the Watch Connectivity session from the iOS app side, it is now time to initialize the session for the WatchKit app. The ideal location in which to place this initialization code is within the *applicationDidFinishLaunching* method of the extension delegate class. Within the Project Navigator panel, select the *ExtensionDelegate.swift* file located under the *WatchConnectApp WatchKit Extension* entry and modify the code to import the WatchConnectivity framework, declare the class as implementing the WCSessionDelegate protocol and to initialize the session:

```swift
import WatchKit
import WatchConnectivity

class ExtensionDelegate: NSObject, WKExtensionDelegate, WCSessionDelegate {
```

```
func applicationDidFinishLaunching() {
    if (WCSession.isSupported()) {
        let session = WCSession.defaultSession()
        session.delegate = self
        session.activateSession()
    }
}
```

13.11 Sending the Message to the iOS app

Now that the WatchKit app user interface is wired up to methods in the interface controller class, the next step is to implement the calls to the *sendMessage* method in those action methods.

Each *sendMessage* method call will include a dictionary consisting of a key named "command" and a value of either "play", "stop" or "volume". In the case of the volume command, an additional key-value pair will be provided within the dictionary with the value set to the current value of the slider. The *sendMessage* method calls will also declare and pass through *replyHandler* and *errorHandler* closures. This is essentially a block of code that will be called and passed data by the iOS application once the message request has been handled.

Within the *InterfaceController.swift* file, implement this code within the action methods so that they read as follows, noting that in each case a check is made to ensure that the iOS app is still reachable:

```
.

.

import WatchConnectivity

.

.

.

@IBAction func startPlay() {
    if WCSession.defaultSession().reachable == true {

        let requestValues = ["command" : "start"]
        let session = WCSession.defaultSession()

        session.sendMessage(requestValues, replyHandler: { reply in
            self.statusLabel.setText(reply["status"] as? String)
            }, errorHandler: { error in
                print("error: \(error)")
        })
    }
}

@IBAction func stopPlay() {
```

```
        if WCSession.defaultSession().reachable == true {

            let requestValues = ["command" : "stop"]
            let session = WCSession.defaultSession()

            session.sendMessage(requestValues, replyHandler: { reply in
                self.statusLabel.setText(reply["status"] as? String)
                }, errorHandler: { error in
                    print("error: \(error)")
            })
        }
    }


    @IBAction func volumeChange(value: Float) {
        let requestValues = ["command" : "volume", "level" : value/10]
        let session = WCSession.defaultSession()

        session.sendMessage(requestValues as! [String : AnyObject],
            replyHandler: { reply in
                self.statusLabel.setText(reply["status"] as? String)
                }, errorHandler: { error in
                    print("error: \(error)")
        })
    }
```

Note that the slider will contain a value between 0 and 10. Since the AVAudioPlayer class has a range of 0.0 to 1.0 for the volume level, the slider value is divided by 10 before being passed to the parent application.

The reply handler closure expects as a parameter a dictionary object. In the case of this example, the closure code simply extracts the string value for the "status" key from the reply dictionary and displays it on the status Label object in the main WatchKit app scene.

13.12 Handling the Message in the iOS app

When the *sendMessage* method is called, the parent iOS application will be notified via a call to the *session:didReceiveMessage:replyHandler* method within the application delegate class. The next step in this tutorial is to implement this method.

Locate and select the *AppDelegate.swift* file in the Project Navigator panel so that it loads into the editor. Once loaded, add an implementation of the *session:didReceiveMessage:replyHandler* method as follows:

```
func session(session: WCSession, didReceiveMessage message: [String :
AnyObject], replyHandler: ([String : AnyObject]) -> Void) {
```

```
var replyValues = Dictionary<String, AnyObject>()

let viewController = self.window!.rootViewController
    as! ViewController

switch message["command"] as! String {
case "start" :
    viewController.startPlay()
    replyValues["status"] = "Playing"
case "stop" :
    viewController.stopPlay()
    replyValues["status"] = "Stopped"
case "volume" :
    let level = message["level"] as! Float
    viewController.adjustVolume(level)
    replyValues["status"] = "Vol = \(level)"
default:
    break
}
replyHandler(replyValues)
}
```

The code begins by creating and initializing a Dictionary instance in which to store the data to be returned to the WatchKit Extension via the reply handler. Next, a reference to the root view controller instance of the iOS app is obtained so that the playback methods in that class can be called later in the method.

One of the arguments passed through to the *session:didReceiveMessage:replyHandler* method is a dictionary named *userInfo*. This is the dictionary that was passed through when the *sendMessage* method was called from the WatchKit app extension (in other words the *requestValues* dictionary declared in the extension action methods). The method uses a switch statement to identify which command has been passed through within this dictionary. Based on the command detected, the corresponding method within the view controller is called. For example, if the "command" key in the *userInfo* dictionary has the string value "play" then the *startPlay* method of the view controller is called to begin audio playback. The value for the "status" key in the *replyValues* dictionary is then configured with the text to be displayed via the status label in the WatchKit app scene.

Also passed through as an argument to the *session:didReceiveMessage:replyHandler* method is a reference to the *reply closure* declared as part of the *sendMessage* method call. The last task performed by the *session:didReceiveMessage:replyHandler* method is to call this closure, passing through the *replyValues* dictionary. As previously described, the reply closure code will then display the status text to the user via the previously declared *statusLabel* outlet.

13.13 **Testing the Application**

In the Xcode toolbar, make sure that the run target menu is set to *WatchConnectApp WatchKit App* before clicking on the run button. Once the WatchKit app appears, click on the Play button in the main interface controller scene. The status label should update to display "Playing" and the music should begin to play within the iOS app. Test that the slider changes the volume and that the Stop button stops the playback. In each case, the response from the parent iOS app should be displayed by the status label.

13.14 **Summary**

This chapter has created an example project intended to demonstrate the use of the WatchConnectivity messaging capabilities to launch and communicate with the iOS companion application of a WatchKit app. The example has shown how to initialize a Watch Connectivity session, call the *sendMessage* method and implement the *session:didReceiveMessage:replyHandler* method within the app delegate of the parent iOS app.

14. An Overview of WatchKit Glances

A WatchKit glance is an optional additional scene intended to provide a quick and lightweight view of the key information provided by a WatchKit app. A WatchKit app can have only one glance scene, which is non-interactive and non-scrollable. Tapping the screen while a glance is displayed opens the corresponding WatchKit app.

This chapter will provide an overview of WatchKit glances. The next chapter, entitled *A WatchKit Glance Tutorial*, will provide a practical implementation of a glance scene for an existing WatchKit app.

14.1 WatchKit Glances

A WatchKit glance is an optional scene that can be added to a WatchKit app. Glances are accessed on the Apple Watch device by performing an upward swipe starting at the bottom of the device display. Glances are displayed in a page-based navigation format allowing the user to swipe left and right to navigate through the glance scenes for the various apps installed on the watch.

WatchKit scenes are intended to show only a subset of the information provided by the WatchKit app and containing iOS app and cannot contain interactive controls such as buttons, sliders or switches. Since glance scenes are non-scrollable it is also essential that the information displayed by the glance fit onto a single screen.

The only user interaction supported in a glance scene is a tap to launch the corresponding WatchKit app. When a WatchKit app is launched via its glance scene, context information can be passed from the glance to the WatchKit app.

A glance should be designed to display the minimum amount of information necessary to inform the user and do so as quickly as possible.

14.2 The Architecture of a WatchKit Glance

A WatchKit glance consists of a scene and a corresponding interface controller derived from the WKInterfaceController class, essentially mirroring the architecture of a standard WatchKit scene. The glance scene is contained within the same storyboard file as all the other scenes within a WatchKit app and the glance interface controller resides within the WatchKit extension.

The lifecycle of the glance interface controller is the same as that of any other interface controller as described in the chapter entitled *An Overview of WatchKit App Architecture*.

A key difference between a glance interface controller and the interface controller for a standard scene is that the operating system will call the initialization lifecycle methods earlier for a glance controller, allowing for a greater amount of time to elapse between the *init* and *awakeWithContext* initialization lifecycle method calls and the call to the *willActivate* lifecycle method immediately before the scene is shown to the user. It is recommended, therefore, that the *willActivate* method be used within glance interface controllers to perform a final check that the information being displayed to the user is still up to date before the scene appears to the user.

14.3 Adding a Glance During WatchKit App Creation

A glance may be added when creating a new *iOS App with WatchKit App* project by selecting the *Include Glance Scene* in the options screen for the new project as shown in Figure 14-1:

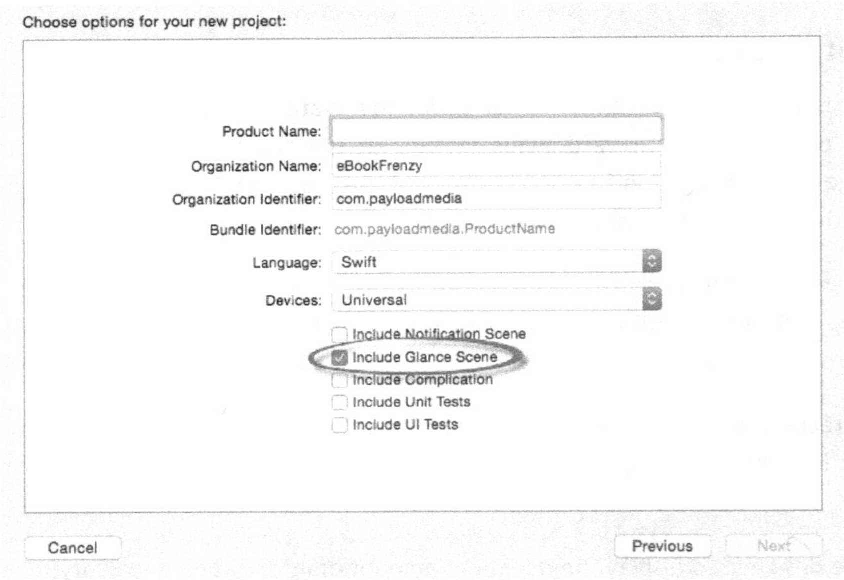

Choose options for your new project:

Product Name:

Organization Name: eBookFrenzy

Organization Identifier: com.payloadmedia

Bundle Identifier: com.payloadmedia.ProductName

Language: Swift

Devices: Universal

☐ Include Notification Scene
☑ Include Glance Scene
☐ Include Complication
☐ Include Unit Tests
☐ Include UI Tests

Cancel   Previous   Next

Figure 14-1

To include a glance when adding a WatchKit app target to an existing iOS project, simply enable the *Include Glance Scene* checkbox in the new target options panel as highlighted in Figure 14-2:

Choose options for your new target:

Product Name:	GlanceDemo
Organization Name:	eBookFrenzy
Organization Identifier:	com.payloadmedia.GlanceDemo
Bundle Identifier:	com.payloadmedia.GlanceDemo.G...
Language:	Swift

    ☐ Include Notification Scene
    ☑ Include Glance Scene
    ☐ Include Complication

Project:	📄 GlanceDemo
Embed in Companion Application:	🅰 GlanceDemo

Cancel   Previous Finish

Figure 14-2

With this option selected, Xcode will add a glance scene to the *Interface.storyboard* file in addition to the standard main scene:

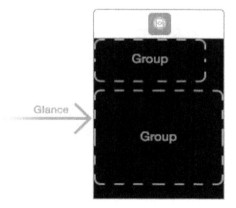

Figure 14-3

In addition to the scene, Xcode will also add a corresponding interface controller source file to the WatchKit extension named *GlanceController.swift* and associate it with the glance storyboard scene.

The last element automatically added to the project by Xcode is a new build scheme configured to compile and run the glance scene. This build scheme appears as an option within the Xcode run target menu as shown in Figure 14-4:

Figure 14-4

14.4 Adding a Glance to an Existing WatchKit App

The inclusion of a glance scene to an existing WatchKit app is a multi-step process that begins with the addition of a Glance Interface Controller scene to the WatchKit app storyboard file. To add the scene, select the *Interface.storyboard* file so that it loads into the Interface Builder tool and drag and drop a *Glance Interface Controller* object from the Object Library panel onto the storyboard canvas (Figure 14-5):

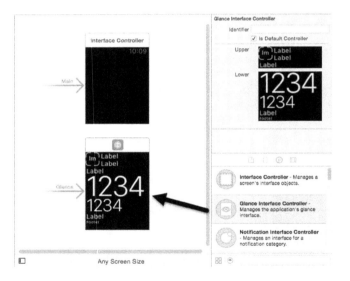

Figure 14-5

Next, add an interface controller to accompany the glance scene by Ctrl-clicking on the WatchKit Extension entry in the Project Navigator panel, selecting the *New File...* menu option and creating a new watchOS WatchKit Class source file subclassed from the WKInterfaceController class.

Return to the *Interface.storyboard* file and select the Glance Interface Controller scene so that it highlights in blue. Display the Identity Inspector panel and select the newly added interface controller class from the *Class* drop-down menu.

The final step is to add a build scheme for the glance scene. The easiest way to achieve this is to duplicate the existing WatchKit App scheme and modify it for the glance scene. Begin this process by selecting the WatchKit App scheme in the run target menu as shown in Figure 14-6:

Figure 14-6

Display the run target menu again, this time selecting the *Edit Scheme…* menu option. Within the scheme editing panel, click on the *Duplicate Scheme* button located in the lower left hand corner and, in the name field located in the upper left hand corner, replace the "Copy of" text with a "Glance – " prefix:

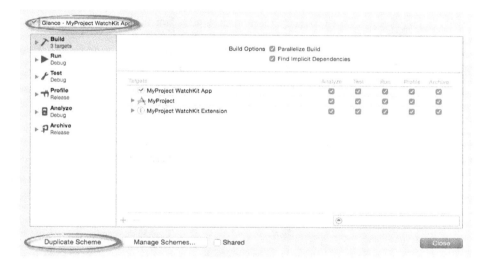

Figure 14-7

With the new scheme created and appropriately named, select the *Run* option on the left hand panel and change the *Watch Interface* option menu in the main panel from *Main* to *Glance* as shown in Figure 14-8:

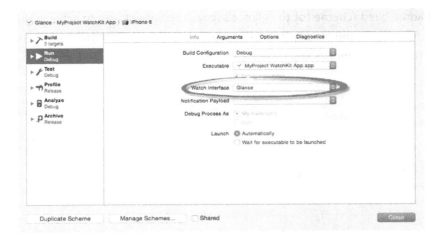

Figure 14-8

With these steps complete the glance is now added and fully integrated into the WatchKit app.

14.5 **WatchKit Glance Scene Layout Templates**

The layout for a WatchKit glance must be based on one of a number of templates provided within the Xcode environment. Glance scenes are divided into upper and lower sections. Xcode currently provides 12 template options for the upper section of the scene and 24 template options for the lower section. The templates vary in the amount of customization that can be performed in terms of adding other visual elements.

To change the template for either the upper or lower section of the scene, select the scene in the storyboard and display the Attributes Inspector in the utilities panel. This will display the current template selections for both sections. Clicking on a section in the panel will display a menu of available alternatives. Figure 14-9, for example, shows the template options for the upper section of the glance scene:

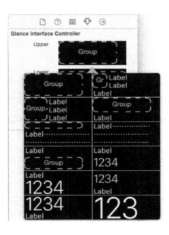

Figure 14-9

14.6 **Passing Context Data to the WatchKit App**

When the user taps a glance scene on the watch display the WatchKit app associated with that glance is launched. In some situations it might be useful to pass some context data from the glance interface controller to the initial interface controller of the WatchKit app. Based on this data the appearance of the WatchKit app can then be changed. A WatchKit app consisting of a number of different scenes might, for example, display a particular scene when launched in this way based on the context data passed through from the glance.

The context data to be passed to the WatchKit app when the user taps on the glance scene is configured by making a call to the *updateUserActivity* method within the glance interface controller. This method takes as parameters a string uniquely identifying the activity, a dictionary object containing the context data and a web page URL. When working with WatchKit glances, only the type string and dictionary parameter are used. The following code, for example, calls the *updateUserActivity* method passing through a dictionary object:

```
updateUserActivity("com.ebookFrenzy.MyProjectApp",
        userInfo: myDictionary, webpageURL: nil)
```

When the WatchKit app launches the *handleUserActivity* method, if implemented in the extension delegate class, will be called and passed the userInfo dictionary object. For example:

```
override func handleUserActivity(userInfo: [NSObject : AnyObject]?) {
        // Extract data from dictionary and handle context
}
```

When called, the *handleUserActivity* method can extract the context data from the dictionary and decide how to tailor the launch of the app in response. This will often require that the extension delegate gain access to the root interface controller of the WatchKit app. A reference to this object can be obtained using the rootInterfaceController property of the WKExtension shared extension object. The following code, for example obtains a reference to the root interface controller from within the extension delegate, makes it the currently active controller and calls a method on that object:

```
let rootController = WKExtension.sharedExtension().rootInterfaceController
                as! InterfaceController

rootController.popToRootController()
rootController.myMethod()
```

14.7 **Summary**

A WatchKit glance is an optional scene that can be added to a WatchKit app. Glances are accessed when the user performs an upward swipe starting at the bottom of the watch display. All of the glances available on the device are displayed using a page-based navigation interface through which the user moves using left and right swiping motions.

The purpose of a glance is to provide quick access to a subset of the information provided by the corresponding WatchKit app. Glance scenes are non-scrollable and do not respond to user interaction with the exception that a tap will launch the corresponding WatchKit app. When the WatchKit app is launched from the glance scene, context data may be passed to the initial interface controller of the WatchKit app.

A glance scene may be created either at the point that a WatchKit app target is added to a project, or added manually to an existing WatchKit app extension. A number of template options are provided within Xcode as the basis for the layout of glance scenes.

Glances are intended to launch and display information quickly. To achieve this, the operating system will "pre-initialize" the glance interface controller by making early calls to the two initialization lifecycle methods. Any last minute updates to the data to be displayed should, therefore, be performed immediately before the scene appears within the *willActivate* method. Tasks that take a long time to complete should be avoided when performing this final update.

15. A WatchKit Glance Tutorial

The tutorial outlined in this chapter will add a glance scene to the TableDemoApp created in the chapter entitled *A WatchKit Table Tutorial* and will make use of the various glance capabilities outlined in the previous chapter, including the addition of a glance to an existing Xcode project and the passing of context data from the glance to the corresponding WatchKit app.

15.1 About the Glance Scene

The TableDemoApp project consists of a table containing a list of workout exercises for a fitness app. When a table row is selected by the user the app navigates to a second scene containing more detailed information about the chosen exercise. In this chapter, a glance scene will be added to this project, the purpose of which is to allow the user to display a summary of the exercise last selected in the WatchKit app. Through the use of context data, tapping the display from within the glance scene will launch the WatchKit app and automatically navigate to the corresponding detail scene.

If you have already completed the TableDemoApp project as outlined in the *A WatchKit Table Tutorial* and *Implementing WatchKit Table Navigation* chapters of this book, open the project in Xcode now. Alternatively, the completed project may be downloaded along with the other sample projects at the following URL:

http://www.ebookfrenzy.com/print/watchos2/index.php

15.2 Adding the Glance to the Project

To add the glance scene to the WatchKit app storyboard, select the *Interface.storyboard* file so that it loads into the Interface Builder tool and drag and drop a *Glance Interface Controller* object from the Object Library panel onto the storyboard canvas (Figure 15-1):

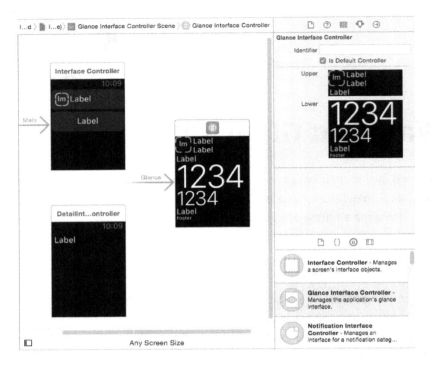

Figure 15-1

With the Glance scene selected in the storyboard, use the Attributes Inspector panel to change both the upper and lower sections of the glance scene to each contain a single Group object containing Image objects as shown in Figure 15-2:

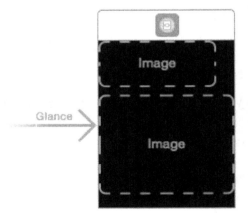

Figure 15-2

Select each of the Image objects and, using the keyboard delete key, remove the objects from the scene leaving behind just the Group objects:

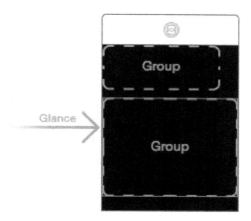

Figure 15-3

Next, add an interface controller to accompany the glance scene by Ctrl-clicking on the *TableDemoApp WatchKit Extension* entry in the Project Navigator panel, selecting the *New File...* menu option and creating a new watchOS Source WatchKit Class file named *GlanceController* and subclassed from the WKInterfaceController class.

Return to the *Interface.storyboard* file and select the Glance Interface Controller scene so that it highlights in blue. Display the Identity Inspector panel and select the newly added interface controller class from the *Class* drop-down menu.

The final step is to add a build scheme for the glance scene by duplicating and modifying the existing WatchKit App scheme. Begin by selecting the WatchKit App scheme in the run target menu as shown in Figure 15-4:

Figure 15-4

Display the run target menu again, this time selecting the *Edit Scheme...* menu option. Within the scheme editing panel, click on the *Duplicate Scheme* button located in the lower left hand corner and, in the name field located in the upper left hand corner, replace the "Copy of" text with a "Glance – " prefix.

With the new scheme created and appropriately named, select the *Run* option on the left hand panel and change the *Watch Interface* option menu in the main panel from *Main* to *Glance* as shown in Figure 15-5:

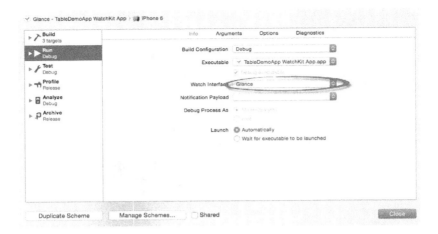

Figure 15-5

Close the panel to commit the changes, at which point the glance is now integrated into the TableDemoApp WatchKit app extension.

15.3 Designing the Glance Scene Layout

The glance scene will use the previously prepared template layout consisting of the two Group interface objects. With the *Interface.storyboard* file displayed within Interface Builder, drag a Label object into each of the group containers within the glance scene as shown in Figure 15-6:

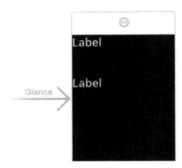

Figure 15-6

Select the Label object in the upper group container, display the Attributes Inspector panel and change the *Vertical* property listed under Alignment to *Center*.

Select the Label object located in the lower group and change both the *Horizontal* and *Vertical* properties in the Alignment section of the panel to *Center*. With the Label object still selected, click on the 'T' icon in the Font property field, change the *Font* menu to *System* and change the *Style* menu to *Bold*. Before clicking on the Done button, increase the *Size* value to 35:

Figure 15-7

On completion of these steps, the layout of the glance scene should match that outlined in Figure 15-8:

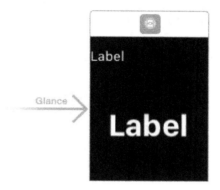

Figure 15-8

15.4 Establishing Outlet Connections

The interface controller for the glance scene will need access to the two labels to change the text that is displayed to the user. Keeping the *Interface.storyboard* file loaded in the Interface Builder tool, display the Assistant Editor panel and make sure that it is displaying the content of the *GlanceController.swift* file. Ctrl-click on the upper label in the glance scene and drag the resulting line to a position immediately beneath the class declaration line in the Assistant Editor panel. Release the line and create an outlet connection named *titleLabel*. Repeat this step to connect the lower label to an outlet named *mainLabel*. At this point the beginning of the *GlanceController.swift* file should read as follows:

```
import WatchKit
import Foundation


class GlanceController: WKInterfaceController {

    @IBOutlet weak var titleLabel: WKInterfaceLabel!
```

```
@IBOutlet weak var mainLabel: WKInterfaceLabel!

override func awakeWithContext(context: AnyObject?) {
    super.awakeWithContext(context)

    // Configure interface objects here.
}
.
.
.
}
```

15.5 Adding Data to the Glance Interface Controller

Now that the user interface of the glance scene is designed and the Label objects are connected to outlets in the interface controller, some data needs to be added to represent the information to be presented when the glance is displayed by the user. The information contained within the glance will consist of the currently selected exercise and a reminder of the duration or number of repetitions to be performed.

Select the *GlanceController.swift* file and add two data arrays to the class so that it reads as follows:

```
import WatchKit
import Foundation

class GlanceController: WKInterfaceController {

    @IBOutlet weak var titleLabel: WKInterfaceLabel!
    @IBOutlet weak var mainLabel: WKInterfaceLabel!

    let titleData = ["Warm-up", "Cardio", "Weightlifting", "Core", "Bike",
"Cooldown"]
    let durationData = ["20 mins", "30 mins", "3 x 10", "2 x 20", "20 mins",
"20 mins"]

    override func awakeWithContext(context: AnyObject?) {
        super.awakeWithContext(context)

        // Configure interface objects here.
    }
.
.
.
}
```

15.6 **Storing and Retrieving the Currently Selected Table Row**

When the glance is invoked by the user it will need to know which row within the corresponding WatchKit app was last selected by the user. The WatchKit app interface controller, therefore, needs to store this information in a location where it can also be accessed by the glance interface controller. Since this is a small amount of data, the ideal location is within user defaults storage using the NSUserDefaults class.

The selection of a table row results in a call to the *didSelectRowAtIndex* method of the main WatchKit app interface controller which now needs to be updated to save the current index value. Within the Project Navigator panel, select the *InterfaceController.swift* file, locate the *didSelectRowAtIndex* method and modify it as follows:

```
override func table(table: WKInterfaceTable, didSelectRowAtIndex rowIndex:
Int) {
    pushControllerWithName("DetailInterfaceController",
        context: detailData[rowIndex-1])

    let userDefaults = NSUserDefaults.standardUserDefaults()
    userDefaults.setObject(rowIndex, forKey: "index")
    userDefaults.synchronize()
}
```

Within the glance interface controller, this stored index value needs to be retrieved and used to display the correct information within the glance scene. Edit the *GlanceController.swift* file and modify the *willActivate* method to update the labels in the scene with the current information:

```
override func willActivate() {
    super.willActivate()

    let userDefaults = NSUserDefaults.standardUserDefaults()
    let index: Int? = userDefaults.integerForKey("index")

    if let arrayIndex = index {
        titleLabel.setText(titleData[arrayIndex - 1])
        mainLabel.setText(durationData[arrayIndex - 1])
    }
}
```

Test that the changes to the project work by running the WatchKit app within the Simulator environment and selecting the Warm-up row from the table so that the detail page appears. Next, within the Xcode toolbar change the run target to the *Glance – TableDemoApp WatchKit App* option and click on the run button. The glance scene should appear and display information relating to the selected Warm-up exercise as illustrated in Figure 15-9:

Figure 15-9

Tapping the glance scene will launch the WatchKit app. Note, however, that the app starts at the table scene and does not automatically navigate to the detail scene for the Warm-up exercise. To address this some code needs to be added to the project to pass context data from the glance to the WatchKit app.

15.7 Passing Context Data to the WatchKit App

As outlined in *An Overview of WatchKit Glances*, a glance interface controller specifies the context data to be passed to the WatchKit app via a call to the *updateUserActivity* method. The ideal location in which to place this method call is within the *willActivate* method of the glance interface controller.

Edit the *GlanceController.swift* file and modify this method as follows:

```
override func willActivate() {
    super.willActivate()

    let userDefaults = NSUserDefaults.standardUserDefaults()
    let index: Int? = userDefaults.integerForKey("index")

    if let arrayIndex = index {
        titleLabel.setText(titleData[arrayIndex - 1])
        mainLabel.setText(durationData[arrayIndex - 1])
        updateUserActivity("com.example.TableDemoApp",
            userInfo: ["controller": arrayIndex], webpageURL: nil)
    }
}
```

The added code calls the *updateUserActivity* method, passing through a dictionary object consisting of a key ("controller") and the current array index value.

When the WatchKit app is launched by a tap on the glance scene, the *handleUserActivity* method of the extension delegate will be called and passed the dictionary object specified when the *updateUserActivity* method was called. This method now needs to be implemented in the *ExtensionDelegate.swift* file, but first a method needs to be added to the *InterfaceController.swift* file that can be called by the *handleUserActivity* to display the appropriate detail scene content. Select the *InterfaceController.swift* file and add this method so that it reads as follows:

```
func displayDetailScene(index: Int) {
    pushControllerWithName("DetailInterfaceController",
            context: detailData[index-1])
}
```

This method accepts an index value and uses it to display the DetailInterfaceController with the appropriate detail content.

Next, add the *handleUserActivity* method to the *ExtensionDelegate.swift* file as follows:

```
func handleUserActivity(userInfo: [NSObject : AnyObject]?) {

    let controllerIndex = userInfo!["controller"] as! Int

    let rootController =
            WKExtension.sharedExtension().rootInterfaceController
                    as! InterfaceController
    rootController.popToRootController()

    rootController.displayDetailScene(controllerIndex)
}
```

The code in the *handleUserActivity* method extracts the index value from the userInfo dictionary, obtains a reference to the root interface controller instance and calls the previously added *displayDetailScene* method on that object passing through the index value as an argument.

Run the WatchKit app once again on the Simulator, this time selecting a different row from the table. Run the glance and tap the screen to launch the WatchKit app. This time, the WatchKit app should launch and display the previously selected detail scene.

Having verified that the code works within the Simulator, install and run the app on a physical Apple Watch device. Once the table appears, select a row and then press the Digital Crown twice to exit the app and display the time. Perform an upward swiping motion on the screen to display the glances and navigate to the table demo glance scene where the title and time should match the row selected in the main WatchKit app. Tapping the glance scene should launch the WatchKit app and automatically navigate to the corresponding detail scene.

If the glance for TableDemoApp does not appear among the glance pages, launch the Watch App on the iPhone and, on the *My Watch* screen, scroll down to and select the TableDemoApp entry. On the resulting settings screen (Figure 15-10), enable the *Show in Glances* option:

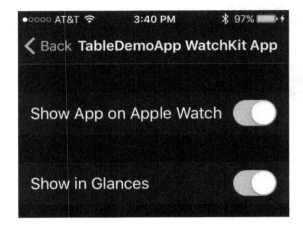

Figure 15-10

15.8 **Summary**

Glances provide a quick way for users to view key information contained within a WatchKit app. This chapter has added a glance scene to the TableDemoApp project, using app group user defaults and context data to pass data back and forth between the glance and the WatchKit app.

Chapter 16

16. A WatchKit Context Menu Tutorial

The Apple Watch display includes touch based technology known as *Force Touch*. A Force Touch event is triggered when the user presses on the screen with slightly more pressure than would be needed to register a tap gesture. When a Force Touch gesture is detected while a WatchKit app is running a context menu will appear if one has been configured.

This chapter will provide an overview of context menus before working through a tutorial involving the use of context menus in a sample WatchKit app.

16.1 An Overview of WatchKit Context Menus

As previously outlined, a context menu appears when the user presses down on the watch display while an app is running. Each storyboard scene within a WatchKit app can have associated with it one context menu.

Each context menu can contain up to four menu items (also referred to as *actions*), each of which is represented by a menu icon. Figure 16-1, for example, shows a context menu containing four menu items:

Figure 16-1

In practical terms, a context menu is actually an instance of the WKInterfaceMenu class while the menu items are represented by instances of the WKInterfaceMenuItem class. Menu items may be added to a context menu within the Interface Builder environment, or added dynamically at runtime from within the code of an interface controller instance. Menu items added dynamically may also be removed at runtime though the same is not true of those added using Interface Builder.

Each menu item needs to be connected to an action method within the interface controller class and will be called when the user taps that item. A tap performed outside any of the menu items dismisses the context menu and returns the user to the app scene.

16.2 Designing Menu Item Images

The icons displayed on menu items may be custom designed or selected from a list of pre-designed icons available from within Xcode. In terms of designing your own menu images some strict rules must be followed.

Each menu item image must be in PNG format and appears as a semi-opaque white circle. Opaque areas of the graphic in the center of the circle always appear in black, with transparent areas allowing the background scene to show through.

For the 38mm Apple Watch the canvas size of the menu image must be 70x70 pixels and for the 42mm device 80x80 pixels.

The background of the image must be fully transparent and must not contain the white circle (this is added automatically by WatchKit). When using a painting or graphic design tool, colors are defined by mixing red, green and blue (RGB) to make other colors. The level of transparency of an RGB-based color is defined by a fourth control referred to as the "Alpha channel" (which combines with RGB to create RGBA). This means that when designing a WatchKit menu image the RGBA alpha channel must be set to zero for the image background so that it is fully transparent. The visible area of the image, on the other hand, is defined by any graphic content that is not entirely transparent.

A sufficient margin must exist between the visible graphic and the outer edge of the white circle. Apple recommends that the non-transparent graphic content of the image not exceed 46x46 pixels and 54x54 pixels for the 38mm and 42mm Apple Watch models respectively. This, however, is only a guideline and it appears that the pre-designed images provided with Xcode use a more generous margin.

Figure 16-2 shows a graphical depiction of a menu image consisting of an opaque circle with a semi-transparent center designed for the 42mm Apple Watch:

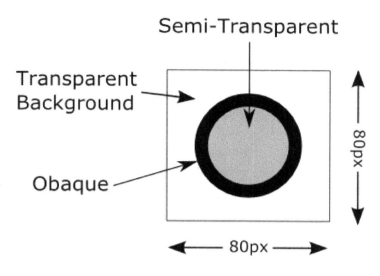

Figure 16-2

16.3 **Creating a Context Menu in Interface Builder**

To add a context menu to a scene in an Interface Builder storyboard simply locate the Menu object in the Object Library panel and drag and drop it onto the scene canvas as outlined in Figure 16-3 below:

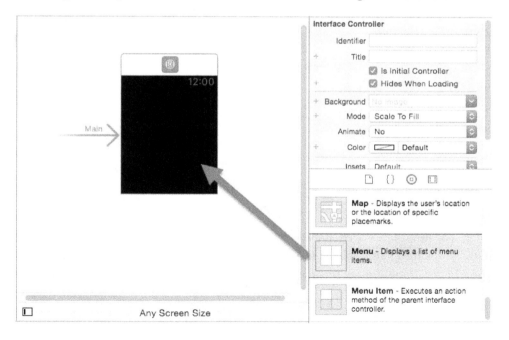

Figure 16-3

Once the menu has been added to the interface controller scene it will not be visible within the scene layout. The only evidence of the presence of the menu can be found in the Document Outline panel (Figure 16-4). As shown in the figure, the menu includes one default menu item when added to a scene:

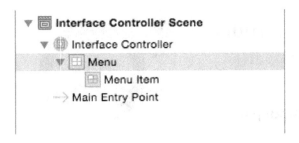

Figure 16-4

Additional menu items are added to the menu by dragging Menu Item objects from the Object Library onto the Menu entry in the Document Outline panel.

Action method connections are established by displaying the Assistant Editor panel, Ctrl-clicking and dragging from a menu item to an appropriate position in the interface controller source file and following the usual steps to establish an action connection.

Select a menu item from the outline panel and display the Attributes Inspector panel (Figure 16-5) to configure the appearance of the menu item.

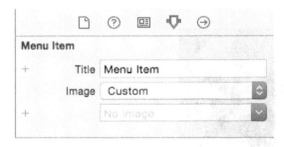

Figure 16-5

The title attribute specifies the text that appears beneath the menu item image circle. If the image menu is set to *Custom*, an image meeting the Apple style guidelines will need to be added to the image assets catalog of the WatchKit App folder in the Project Navigator panel and then selected from the drop down menu located beneath the Image menu.

To select a pre-defined image, simply click on the *Image* menu and make a selection:

Figure 16-6

16.4 **Adding and Removing Menu Items in Code**

If a context menu has been added to a WatchKit storyboard scene, additional menu items may be added dynamically within the code of the interface controller using the following interface controller methods:

- **addMenuItemWithImage** – Takes as parameters a UIImage object containing the image to be displayed, the title string to display beneath the image and a reference to the method to be called when the item is selected.

- **addMenuItemWithImageNamed** – This method is used when the image to be displayed is already included in the WatchKit app resources. The method takes as parameters the name of the image file stored on the Apple Watch device, the title string to be displayed beneath the image and a reference to the method to be called when the item is selected.

- **addMenuItemWithIcon** – Allows one of the pre-designed template icons to be specified for the menu item image. In addition to the icon reference, this method also requires the title string to be displayed beneath the image and a reference to the method to be called when the item is selected.

When calling the *addMenuItemWithIcon* method, the icon options are defined within the *WKMenuItemIcon* enumeration and may be referenced as follows:

```
WKMenuItemIcon.Accept
WKMenuItemIcon.Add
WKMenuItemIcon.Block
WKMenuItemIcon.Decline
WKMenuItemIcon.Info
```

```
WKMenuItemIcon.Maybe
WKMenuItemIcon.More
WKMenuItemIcon.Mute
WKMenuItemIcon.Pause
WKMenuItemIcon.Play
WKMenuItemIcon.Repeat
WKMenuItemIcon.Resume
WKMenuItemIcon.Share
WKMenuItemIcon.Shuffle
WKMenuItemIcon.Speaker
WKMenuItemIcon.Trash
```

The following code, for example, adds a menu item to a context menu using the "Pause" template icon configured to call an action method named *pauseSelected*:

```
addMenuItemWithItemIcon(WKMenuItemIcon.Pause, title: "Pause",
                        action: "pauseSelected")
```

All of the menu items added from within the interface controller code may be removed via a call to the *clearAllMenuItems* method of the interface controller object. Any menu items added to the storyboard scene using Interface Builder are unaffected by this method call.

16.5 Creating the Context Menu Example Project

Start Xcode and create a new iOS project. On the template screen choose the *Application* option located under *watchOS* in the left hand panel and select *iOS App with WatchKit App*. Click *Next,* set the product name to *ContextMenu,* enter your organization identifier and make sure that the *Devices* menu is set to *Universal.* Before clicking *Next,* change the *Language* menu to Swift and switch off all of the *Include* options. On the final screen, choose a location in which to store the project files and click on *Create* to proceed to the main Xcode project window.

16.6 Designing the WatchKit App User Interface

When the project is complete, the WatchKit app will include a user interface comprising four menu items. When a menu item is selected, the text displayed on a Label object in the main scene will change to reflect the selected option. Select the *Interface.storyboard* file in the Project Navigator panel and drag and drop a Label interface object from the Object Library onto the main storyboard scene. With the newly added Label object selected, display the Attributes Inspector panel and change the *Horizontal* and *Vertical* Alignment properties to *Center* at which point the scene should match Figure 16-7:

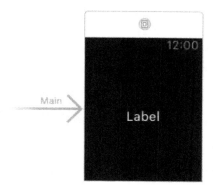

Figure 16-7

Display the Assistant Editor and verify that it is displaying the content of the *InterfaceController.swift* file. Ctrl-click on the Label object in the scene and drag the resulting line to a position immediately beneath the class declaration line in the Assistant Editor panel. Release the line and establish an outlet connection named *statusLabel*.

16.7 Designing the Context Menu

Remaining within the *Interface.storyboard* file, drag a Menu object from the Object Library and drop it onto the main scene as previously illustrated in Figure 16-3. Display the Document Outline panel using the button in the bottom left hand corner of the Interface Builder panel (indicated in Figure 16-8) and select the first Menu Item located beneath the Menu entry:

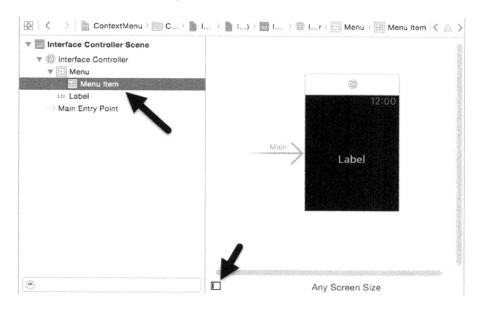

Figure 16-8

Display the Attributes Inspector and change the *Image* menu setting to *Play* and enter Play into the Title field.

Drag and drop three more Menu Item objects from the Object Library onto the *Menu* entry in the Document Outline panel, changing the *Image* property in the Attributes Inspector for each one to *Pause*, *Block* and *Shuffle* respectively. While configuring images, change the Title field for each Menu Item to Pause, Stop and Shuffle.

16.8 Establishing the Action Connections

Display the Assistant Editor, Ctrl-click on the uppermost Menu Item entry in the Document Outline panel and drag the line to a position beneath the *willActivate* method in the editor panel. Release the line and establish an action connection to a method named *playSelected*.

Repeat these steps for the remaining three Menu Items, connecting them to action methods named *pauseSelected*, *stopSelected* and *shuffleSelected*.

Next, edit the *InterfaceController.swift* file and implement the code in the four action method stubs to read as follows:

```
@IBAction func playSelected() {
    statusLabel.setText("Play")
}

@IBAction func pauseSelected() {
    statusLabel.setText("Pause")
}

@IBAction func stopSelected() {
    statusLabel.setText("Stop")
}

@IBAction func shuffleSelected() {
    statusLabel.setText("Shuffle")
}
```

16.9 Testing the Context Menu App

Compile and run the WatchKit app and when the app is running, press firmly on the device screen to invoke the context menu (to perform a deep press on the Watch Simulator, select the *Hardware -> Force Touch Pressure -> Deep Press* menu option, click on the screen then switch back to *Shallow Press* mode). The context menu should appear as illustrated in Figure 16-9:

Figure 16-9

Selecting a menu item from the menu should dismiss the context menu and change the text on the Label object in the main scene to match the menu item selection.

16.10 Summary

The Force Touch technology built into the display of the Apple Watch is able to differentiate between a tap and a more forceful pressing motion on the device screen. When a force touch is detected by the device when an app is running the context menu associated with the current scene will be displayed. Each scene within a WatchKit app can have a single context menu, each of which can present up to four menu items available for selection by the user. Each menu item consists of an image and a title.

17. Working with Images in WatchKit

There are a number of factors that need to be taken into consideration when working with images within a WatchKit app such as whether the image can be included within the WatchKit app bundle or WatchKit extension, or needs to be transferred from the iPhone to the Apple Watch device at runtime. Unlike iPhone based apps, the size of the images used within a WatchKit app is also of key importance, particularly when working with large image files.

The goal of this chapter is to explore the various options for managing and displaying images in a WatchKit app including topics such as image caching, named images, animation, image compression, asset catalogs and image templates.

17.1 Displaying Images in WatchKit Apps

WatchKit provides two ways in which images can be displayed within a WatchKit app. The first involves the use of the WKInterfaceImage interface object class. When added to the scene of a WatchKit app storyboard, this object can be used to display images to the user. Another option involves setting an image as a background on the WKInterfaceGroup, WKInterfaceButton and WKInterfaceController classes. In both scenarios, the image can be specified within the storyboard file or set dynamically from within the code of the interface controller at runtime.

Wherever possible, images should be in PNG or JPEG format and sized to match the display size of the interface object on which they are to be displayed. Whilst WatchKit is able to handle other image formats, Apple warns that app performance is likely to be impacted adversely when those images are rendered.

Images can be generated and stored within the WatchKit extension or included as part of the WatchKit app or extension bundle.

17.2 Images Originating in the WatchKit Extension

Whenever a UIImage object is created or included within the extension of a WatchKit app, that image is local to the extension. The image contained within a UIImage object in a WatchKit extension can be displayed using the *setImage*, *setImageData*, *setBackgroundImage* and *setBackgroundImageData* methods of the interface object on which the image is to be displayed. The following code, for example, displays an image stored within a WatchKit extension onto a WKInterfaceImage object via an outlet connection named *myImage*:

```
let theImage = UIImage(named: "spaceship")
myImage.setImage(theImage)
```

An alternative to including images as part of the WatchKit App extension is to include image files as part of the WatchKit app bundle. Such images are referred to as *named images*.

17.3 **Understanding Named Images**

Images that are bundled with the WatchKit app bundle are referred to as *named images* and are displayed using the *setImageNamed* and *setBackgroundImageNamed* methods of the interface objects on which the image is to be displayed. The following code, for example, displays a named image as the background for a WKInterfaceGroup object instance:

```
myGroup.setBackgroundImageNamed("spaceship")
```

17.4 **Adding Images to a WatchKit App**

Images can be stored as part of the WatchKit app bundle or WatchKit extension by placing them in the target's *Assets.xcassets* asset catalog. Figure 17-1, for example, highlights the image assets catalogs for WatchKit app and WatchKit extension targets within the Xcode project navigator panel:

Figure 17-1

When files are stored into the image asset catalog the file names must end with "@2x", for example *myimage@2x.png*. This indicates to the asset catalog that the images are suitable for display on the retina screen of the Apple Watch device family. For the purposes of an example, assume that we have a file named *spaceship@2x.png* and need to add this as a named image to the WatchKit app bundle image asset catalog. The first step would be to select the *Assets.xcassets* catalog entry in the WatchKit app target as shown in Figure 17-2:

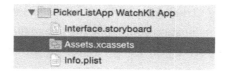

Figure 17-2

Making this selection will load the catalog into the main Xcode panel:

Figure 17-3

The left hand panel lists the *image sets* that are currently contained within the catalog. An image set collects together images in different sizes and resolutions. By default, the image asset catalog for a WatchKit app target contains a single image set named *AppIcon*. As the name suggests, this image set contains the icon used to represent the WatchKit app in a variety of locations such as the home screen and notification center.

To create a new image set for an image, simply locate the image in a Finder window and drag and drop it onto the image set panel as illustrated in Figure 17-4:

Figure 17-4

Multiple images may be imported by Ctrl-clicking within the image set panel, selecting the *Import...* menu option and navigating to the file system location containing the image files. If a folder is selected for import, all of the images in that folder will be imported into a single image set with a name reflecting that of the selected folder.

Once the image has been added, a new image set will be listed containing the 2x image. If this were an image set for an iOS app it would also be recommended to add 1x (for non-retina screens) and 3x (for iPhone 6 Plus and iPad devices) images to the image set. Since the Apple Watch has retina-only displays of similar sizes only the 2x image is required:

Figure 17-5

When referencing an image stored in an asset catalog, the "@2x" is dropped from the filename. With the image file named *spaceship@2x.png* contained in an image asset catalog for a WatchKit app target, the code to display this image on a WKInterfaceImage object would read as follows:

```
myImage.setImageNamed("spaceship")
```

17.5 Compressing Large Images

Depending on the image size, it can take a considerable amount of time to transfer an image from the iPhone to the Apple Watch. Consider a scenario in which the extension for a WatchKit app needs to display a photo that the user has taken using the iPhone camera. Transferring such an image could take over two minutes to transfer wirelessly from the iPhone to the watch. This is clearly an unacceptable amount of time to keep the user waiting.

In reality the image that is taken by the iPhone camera is orders of magnitude larger than is necessary to fit on the display of an Apple Watch. In fact, an image from the iPhone camera roll is measured in thousands of pixels while the display of even the largest Apple Watch model has a resolution of only 312 x 390 pixels. Clearly there is significant opportunity for reducing the size of any large images before they are transferred to the Apple Watch for display.

There are a number of options for reducing the size of any images both in terms of dimensions and storage space before the transfer to the watch takes place. The following code, for example, is useful for reducing the size of an image by a specified scale factor:

```
if let largeImage = UIImage(named: "myLargeImage") {

    let imageSize = largeImage.size
    let scale: CGFloat = 0.15 // Scale factor

    let reducedSize = CGSizeMake(imageSize.width * scale,
            imageSize.height * scale);

    UIGraphicsBeginImageContext(reducedSize)

    largeImage.drawInRect(CGRectMake(0, 0, reducedSize.width,
            reducedSize.height))

    let compressedImage = UIGraphicsGetImageFromCurrentImageContext()

    UIGraphicsEndImageContext()
    myImage.setImage(compressedImage) // Display the image
}
```

In tests on an original PNG image file of 2448 x 3264 pixels with a size of 23MB the transfer time was reduced from approximately 3 minutes down to just 6 seconds after the image was compressed using the above code.

17.6 Specifying the WKInterfaceImage Object Dimensions in Code

When a WKInterfaceImage interface object is added to a storyboard scene using Interface Builder the dimensions of the object can be specified from within the Attributes Inspector panel (Figure 17-6). Options are available to allow the object to resize to accommodate the assigned image content, to size relative to the container in which the interface object is located, or to specify fixed height and width dimensions:

Figure 17-6

It is also possible to specify fixed height and width properties for a WKInterfaceImage object from within the code of the corresponding interface controller class. This involves establishing an outlet connection to the image object and making calls to the *setHeight* and *setWidth* methods of that instance, for example:

```
myImage.setHeight(100)
myImage.setWidth(170)
```

17.7 Displaying Animated Images

The WKInterfaceImage interface object is able to display animated images. This animation takes the form of a sequence of images with each image representing a single frame of the animation. To create an animation sequence, the image files should be added to the project (preferably bundled with the WatchKit app as named images) using a file naming convention of *name<sequence number>@2x.png* (for example animation0@2x.png, animation1@2x.png, animation2@2x.png and so on).

The way in which the sequence of animation images is converted into a single animation image and displayed to the user depends on whether the images are bundled with the WatchKit app as named images (the recommended approach for better performance), or reside within the extension.

If the animation images are bundled as named images within the WatchKit app, the animated image can be created and displayed using the *setImageNamed* method of the WKInterfaceImage instance, passing through the image file name prefix. Assuming a set of animation images named animation<*image number*>.png bundled with the WatchKit app, the animation would be displayed on a WKInterfaceImage instance with a single line of code as follows:

```
myImage.setImageNamed("animation")
```

When executed, the above method call collects together all of the appropriately named animation sequence images and uses them to create a single animated UIImage object which is then displayed on the corresponding WKInterfaceImage object.

In the case of extension-based animation images, an animated UIImage object must first be created using the *animatedImageNamed* method of the UIImage class which is then assigned to the WKInterfaceImage object via the object's *setImage* method. For example:

```
let animatedImage = UIImage.animatedImageNamed("animation",
         duration: 20)

myImage.setImage(animatedImage)
```

Once the animated image has been displayed, the *startAnimating* method of the WKInterfaceImage object can be used to begin the animation:

```
myImage.startAnimating()
```

The animation may be customized in terms of duration, repetition and the range of images used within the animation sequence using the *startAnimatingWithImagesInRange* method. The following code customizes an animation to use images from positions 1 through 4 of the image sequence with a 6 second duration and 2 repetitions:

```
myImage.startAnimatingWithImagesInRange(NSRange(location: 1,
                 length: 4), duration: 6, repeatCount: 2)
```

An animation sequence may be stopped at any time via a call to the *stopAnimating* method:

```
myImage.stopAnimating()
```

The implementation of animation within a WatchKit app will be covered in greater detail in the next chapter entitled *A WatchKit Animated Image Tutorial*.

17.8 **Template Images and Tinting**

Images contained within an image asset catalog may be designated as *template images*. When an image is configured as a template image all color information in the image is ignored and the graphic displayed is defined by the stencil that is created by the transparent areas of the image in relation to the non-transparent areas. In Figure 17-7, for example, the rocket image is drawn against a transparent background:

Figure 17-7

When configured as a template image, the colored, non-transparent area of the image is filled with a solid color (light blue by default) creating the stencil image shown in Figure 17-8:

Figure 17-8

To specify that an image is to be rendered as a template, select the image in the asset catalog, display the Attributes Inspector panel and change the *Render As* menu to *Template Image*:

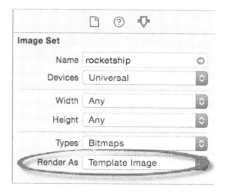

Figure 17-9

The default blue color used for the solid area of the image can be defined within Interface Builder by selecting the interface object on which the image is to be displayed and changing the *Tint* color setting. A tint color may also be assigned from within the interface controller code using the *setTintColor* method of the interface object, for example:

```
myImage.setTintColor(UIColor.redColor())
```

17.9 Summary

Images can be displayed within a WatchKit app scene either using an instance of the WKInterfaceImage class, or as a background image for WKInterfaceButton and WKInterfaceGroup classes. Images included in the WatchKit app bundle and WatchKit extension are pre-installed on the Apple Watch device along with the app. It is important to remember that those installed with the WatchKit app bundle are referred to as *named images* and are accessed differently in code compared to those located within the extension.

In addition to static images, WatchKit also provides support for animated images, an example of which will be demonstrated in the next chapter.

Chapter 18

18. A WatchKit Animated Image Tutorial

The previous chapter touched briefly on the subject of animated images within the context of a WatchKit app. This chapter will expand on this knowledge through the implementation of an example application that creates and displays an animated image within a WatchKit app scene.

18.1 Creating the Animation Example Project

Start Xcode and create a new iOS project. On the template screen choose the *Application* option located under *watchOS* in the left hand panel and select *iOS App with WatchKit App*. Click *Next,* set the product name to *AnimationApp,* enter your organization identifier and make sure that the *Devices* menu is set to *Universal*. Before clicking *Next*, change the *Language* menu to Swift and switch off all of the *Include* options. On the final screen, choose a location in which to store the project files and click on *Create* to proceed to the main Xcode project window.

18.2 Designing the Main Scene Layout

The only interface object required within the main WatchKit app scene is an Image object. Within the Xcode project navigator panel, locate and select the *Interface.storyboard* file so that it loads into the Interface Builder environment. Once loaded, locate the Image object in the Object Library panel and drag and drop it onto the main storyboard scene. With the newly added image object selected, display the Attributes Inspector and change both the *Horizontal* and *Vertical* Alignment properties to *Center* so that the scene layout matches Figure 18-1:

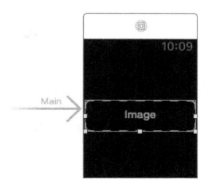

Figure 18-1

Display the Assistant Editor panel and establish an outlet connection from the Image object in the scene named *imageObject*.

18.3 Adding the Animation Sequence Images

The animation sequence in this example consists of 40 PNG image files, which combine to make up an animation of the planet Earth rotating. These files can be found in the *animation_images* folder of the sample code archive, available for download from the following link:

http://www.ebookfrenzy.com/print/watchos2/index.php

Locate and select the *Assets.xcassets* entry listed under the *AnimationApp WatchKit App* folder within the Xcode Project Navigator panel. Ctrl-click in the left hand panel of the asset catalog and select the *Import...* option from the resulting menu. Within the file selection dialog, navigate to and select the *animation_images* folder and click on *Open*.

Once the images have been imported into the asset catalog a new image set will be created named *animation_images* containing all of the animation sequence images:

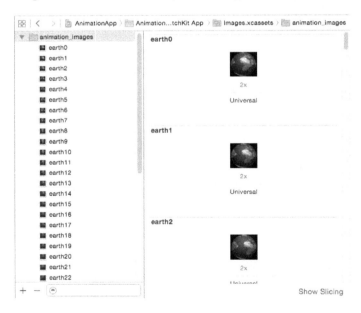

Figure 18-2

With the images added to the asset catalog, all that remains is to add some code in the interface controller class to create and initiate the animation.

18.4 Creating and Starting the Animated Image

Locate and edit the *InterfaceController.swift* file and modify the *awakeWithContext* method to create and display the animation image:

```
override func awakeWithContext(context: AnyObject?) {
    super.awakeWithContext(context)

    imageObject.setImageNamed("earth")
}
```

Compile and run the WatchKit app and note that image 0 appears but that the image object does not animate through the remaining frames. Modify the code further to start the animation sequence:

```
override func awakeWithContext(context: AnyObject?) {
    super.awakeWithContext(context)

    imageObject.setImageNamed("animation")
    imageObject.startAnimating()
}
```

When the app is re-launched the image object will now cycle rapidly and repeatedly through the animation frames showing the Earth rotating. To slow the animation down, the *startAnimating* method can be replaced with a call to the *startAnimatingWithImagesInRange* method specifying a duration, repeat count and a range that encompasses all of the images in the animation:

```
override func awakeWithContext(context: AnyObject?) {
    super.awakeWithContext(context)

    imageObject.setImageNamed("animation")
    imageObject.startAnimatingWithImagesInRange(NSRange(location: 0,
        length: 40), duration: 7, repeatCount: 2)
}
```

When the app is now run, the animation frames will be run more slowly so that the entire sequence takes 7 seconds to complete. The animation should also now stop after 2 repetitions. To configure the animation loop to repeat indefinitely simply change the *repeatCount* value to 0.

Figure 18-3

18.5 **Summary**

This chapter created a sample project that demonstrates the implementation of animated images within a WatchKit app. The tutorial covered the steps required to add animation sequence images to a WatchKit app target in Xcode and outlined the code required within the interface controller to convert those images to an animated image and display that animation to the user. The chapter also explored the different ways in which the animation may be customized in terms of duration, repetition and frame range.

19. WatchKit Dynamic Layout Changes and Animation

Although the initial layout of a WatchKit app scene is defined at design time from within the Interface Builder environment, this does not mean that dynamic changes cannot be made to certain aspects of the appearance of the objects in the scene during runtime. A number of API calls have been introduced with watchOS 2 that allow the size, position and appearance of the interface objects in a scene to be changed dynamically from within the code of the running app. It is now possible, for example, to change the position and size of an object in a scene from within the code of an interface controller.

watchOS 2 also includes the ability to animate some of the property changes made to the interface objects in a scene allowing, for example, an object to slide slowly from one position on the screen to another.

Both dynamic layout changes and animation are the topics of this chapter.

19.1 Changing the Position of an Interface Object

The vertical position of an interface object can be changed via a call to the object's *setVerticalAlignment* method, passing through one of the following values:

- WKInterfaceObjectVerticalAlignment.Top
- WKInterfaceObjectVerticalAlignment.Center
- WKInterfaceObjectVerticalAlignment.Bottom

Similarly, the horizontal position of an interface object may be changed via a call to the object's *setHorizontalAlignment* method using one of the following values:

- WKInterfaceObjectHorizontalAlignment.Left
- WKInterfaceObjectHorizontalAlignment.Center
- WKInterfaceObjectHorizontalAlignment.Right

The following code, for example, sets top and left alignment properties on an interface object referenced by an outlet named myObject:

```
myObject.setHorizontalAlignment(.Left)
myObject.setVerticalAlignment(.Top)
```

19.2 Changing the Size of an Interface Object

The size of an interface object may be set in terms of width and height. Options are available to set these dimensions based on specific dimension values or as a percentage of the size of the container in which the object resides. Interface objects may also be configured to be sized to fit content.

Specific width and height settings are applied to an interface object using the *setHeight* and *setWidth* methods. For example:

```
myObject.setWidth(10)
myObject.setHeight(10)
```

Size changes relative to the width of the container are made using the *setRelativeHeight* and *setRelativeWidth* methods. The values are declared as a percentage and may also include a positive or negative offset value in points.

The following line of code sets the width of an interface object to 60% of the width of the container:

```
myObject.setRelativeWidth(0.6, withAdjustment: 0)
```

The following code, on the other hand, sets the height of an interface object to 30% of the container's width with an adjustment of -20 points:

```
myObject.setRelativeHeight(0.3, withAdjustment: -20)
```

Finally, an interface object may be configured such that it sizes to fit its content using the *sizeToFitWidth* and *sizeToFitHeight* methods:

```
myObject.sizeToFitHeight()
myObject.sizeToFitWidth()
```

19.3 Setting the Visibility of an Interface Object

The visibility of an interface object can be changed from within code via a call to the object's *setHidden* method:

```
myObject.setHidden(true)
myObject.setHidden(false)
```

The transparency of an interface object is adjusted using the *setAlpha* method, passing through a value between 0.0 and 1.0 with 1.0 representing a fully opaque appearance:

```
myObject.setAlpha(0.5)
```

19.4 **Animating Interface Changes**

The concept of animation within the scene of a WatchKit app involves the use of so-called *animation block* methods. Animation block methods are used to mark the beginning and end of a sequence of changes to the appearance of interface objects within a scene. Once the end of the block is reached, the animation is performed over a specified duration. For the sake of example, consider a Button object connected to an outlet named *myButton.* The application requires that the button gradually fade from view over a period of 3 seconds. This can be achieved by making the button transparent through the use of the *alpha* property:

```
myButton.setAlpha = 0
```

Simply setting the alpha property to 0, however, causes the button to immediately become transparent. In order to make it fade out of sight gradually we need to place this line of code in a call to the *animateWithDuration:* animation block method as follows:

```
self.animateWithDuration(3.0, animations: {
    self.myButton.setAlpha(0.0)
})
```

When the above code is executed, the object will gradually fade from view over a period of 3 seconds.

19.5 **Animation and Interface Controller Lifecycle Methods**

If animation is to begin as soon as a storyboard scene is made visible to the user, it is recommended that the animation initialization code be placed within the *didAppear* lifecycle method of the corresponding interface controller class. Similarly, code to stop any currently running animations should be placed within the interface controller's *willDisappear* lifecycle method.

19.6 **An Animation Example**

Start Xcode and create a new iOS project. On the template screen choose the *Application* option located under *watchOS* in the left hand panel and select *iOS App with WatchKit App.* Click *Next,* set the product name to *AnimateInterfaceApp,* enter your organization identifier and make sure that the *Devices* menu is set to *Universal.* Before clicking *Next*, change the *Language* menu to Swift and switch off all of the *Include* options. On the final screen, choose a location in which to store the project files and click on *Create* to proceed to the main Xcode project window.

19.7 **Designing the User Interface**

Select the *Interface.storyboard* file located under *AnimateInterfaceApp WatchKit App* so that it loads into Interface Builder. Locate the Group object in the Object Library panel and drag and drop it onto the scene in the storyboard canvas.

With the Group object selected, display the Attributes Inspector panel and set the background color to a light shade of blue. Set both the width and height size properties to *Relative to container* with values set to 0.3 as illustrated in Figure 19-1:

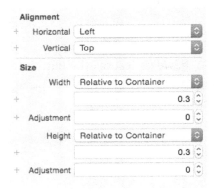

Figure 19-1

Drag and drop a Button object onto the scene and use the Attributes Inspector panel to change the Vertical Alignment property to position the object at the bottom of the scene. Double click on the Button object and change the text to read "Animate". On completion of these steps the user interface layout should resemble that of Figure 19-2:

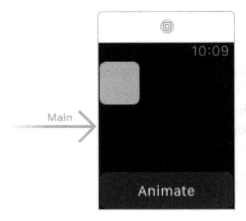

Figure 19-2

Display the Assistant Editor panel and establish an outlet connection from the Group object named *myGroup* and an action connection from the Button object named *changeLayout*.

19.8 Performing the Layout Changes and Animation

Locate and select the *InterfaceController.swift* file and modify the *changeLayout* method to animate a sequence of changes to the size, position and color of the Group object in the scene layout over a 3 second duration:

```
@IBAction func changeLayout() {
    self.animateWithDuration(3.0, animations: {

        self.myGroup.setRelativeWidth(0.7, withAdjustment: 0)
        self.myGroup.setRelativeHeight(0.5, withAdjustment: 0)
        self.myGroup.setHorizontalAlignment(.Right)
        self.myGroup.setVerticalAlignment(.Bottom)
        self.myGroup.setBackgroundColor(UIColor.redColor())
    })
}
```

19.9 Testing the Animation

Compile and run the app on an Apple Watch or using the Watch Simulator and tap the Animate button at which point the Group object should smoothly move to the bottom right hand corner as it gradually increases in size and changes color from blue to red:

Figure 19-3

19.10 Summary

Although the user interface layout for a WatchKit app scene needs to be pre-designed statically within Interface Builder, a number of mechanisms are available for making dynamic changes to interface objects once the app is running. Changes such as the size, alignment and transparency of the interface objects within a scene can all be made from within the code of an interface controller class. The animation features of watchOS 2 can also be used to animate the changes as they are made to the layout of a scene.

20. Working with Fonts and Attributed Strings in WatchKit

Fonts are an important part of making a WatchKit app visually appealing and accessible to the user. WatchKit provides three options when making choices about the fonts to use within the scene of an app. These options consist of text style fonts, system fonts and custom fonts. The subject of custom fonts will be covered in detail in the next chapter entitled *A WatchKit App Custom Font Tutorial*. This chapter, however, will introduce the concepts of text styles and system fonts and outline how these can be used both from within Interface Builder and, through the use of attributed strings, via the code of an interface controller class.

20.1 Dynamic Text and Text Style Fonts

Apple Watch users are able to specify a preferred text size which WatchKit apps are expected to adopt when displaying text (also referred to as the *preferred content size*). The current text size can be configured via the Apple Watch app on the paired iPhone device. To access this setting, launch the Apple Watch app, select the *My Watch* tab followed by the *Brightness & Text Size* option. As shown in Figure 20-1, options are provided on this screen to adjust the font size and use bold text.

Almost without exception, the built-in WatchKit apps adopt the font size setting selected by the user when displaying text. Apple also recommends that third-party apps conform to the user's text size selection wherever possible. WatchKit specifies a variety of different preferred text styles for this purpose including headings, sub-headings, body, captions and footnotes. The text style used by an interface object in a scene can be configured either using Interface Builder or in code.

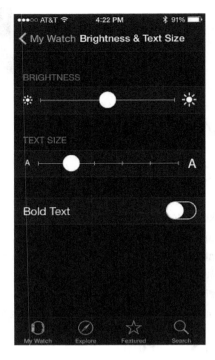

Figure 20-1

To configure the text style of an interface object in Interface Builder, select the interface object to which the style is to be applied, display the Attributes Inspector and click on the "T" button in the Font setting field. From the drop-down menu click on the Font menu button and select an item from the options listed under the *Text Styles* heading:

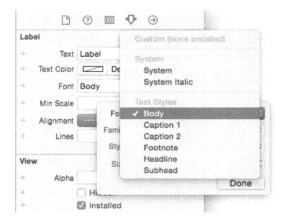

Figure 20-2

When the app is run, the text on the interface object on which the font setting was made will be displayed using the font for the selected text style and sized according to the user's preferred content size category setting.

Behind the scenes, the text style selections are translated to fonts from Apple's San Francisco Font Family. The Headline text style, for example, is displayed using the San Francisco Text font.

20.2 Using Text Style Fonts in Code

A text style font may be retrieved and used from within the code of an interface controller class using the *preferredFontForTextStyle* method of the UIFont class, passing through one of the following pre-configured text style values:

- UIFontTextStyleHeadline
- UIFontTextStyleSubheadline
- UIFontTextStyleBody
- UIFontTextStyleFootnote
- UIFontTextStyleCaption1
- UIFontTextStyleCaption2

The following code, for example, retrieves a Headline text style font object:

```
let headlineFont =
    UIFont.preferredFontForTextStyle(UIFontTextStyleHeadline)
```

When executed, the above code will request the preferred headline style font from the system. The method call will return a UIFont object configured with the headline font sized to match the user's current preferred content size category setting.

Having obtained the preferred font, the next step is to use the font to render the text displayed on a Label or Button interface object. As will be outlined in the next section, this involves the use of *attributed strings*.

20.3 Understanding Attributed Strings

To display text within a WatchKit app using a particular font it is necessary to use an attributed string. Attributed strings are represented using the NSAttributedString and NSMutableAttributedString classes and allow text to be combined with attributes such as fonts and colors.

Having obtained a font object as outlined in the previous section, the next task is to create a Dictionary object with a key set to *NSFontAttributeName* and the font object as the value. This dictionary is then used to specify the attributes for an NSAttributedString instance. The following code, for example, obtains a font object for the headline text style and uses it to create an attributed string that reads "Apple Watch":

```
let headlineFont =
    UIFont.preferredFontForTextStyle(UIFontTextStyleHeadline)
```

```
let fontAttribute = [NSFontAttributeName : headlineFont]

let attributedString = NSAttributedString(string: "Apple Watch",
            attributes: fontAttribute)
```

Once an attributed string has been created, it can be applied to Button and Label interface objects using the *setAttributedTitle* and *setAttributedText* methods respectively. The following code, for example, displays the *attributedString* text from the above example on a Label object:

```
myLabel.setAttributedText(attributedString)
```

When executed, text which reads "Apple Watch" will be rendered on the label referenced by the *myLabel* outlet using the headline font style sized according to the user's preferred content size setting as shown in Figure 20-3:

Figure 20-3

The above example uses an attributed string to set one attribute for the entire text string. In practice, attributed strings can contain multiple attributes covering different ranges of characters within the string. Multiple attributes within an attributed string require the use of the NSMutableAttributedString class. Once an instance of this class has been created and initialized with a string, the *addAttribute* method may be called to add attributes for ranges of characters in the string. For the purposes of the example project, this approach will be used to change the colors used to render the words "Apple" and "Watch" in the label in Figure 20-3. The code to achieve this reads as follows:

```
let headlineFont =
        UIFont.preferredFontForTextStyle(UIFontTextStyleHeadline)

let fontAttribute = [NSFontAttributeName : headlineFont]

let attributedText = NSMutableAttributedString(
```

```
                              string: "Apple Watch",
                              attributes: fontAttribute)

let firstRange = NSRange(location: 0, length: 5)
let secondRange = NSRange(location: 6, length: 5)

attributedText.addAttribute(
                      NSForegroundColorAttributeName,
                      value: UIColor.greenColor(),
                      range: firstRange)

attributedText.addAttribute(
                      NSForegroundColorAttributeName,
                      value: UIColor.redColor(),
                      range: secondRange)

myLabel.setAttributedText(attributedText)
```

The above code creates a mutable attributed string using the headline text style font. Two range objects are then created and initialized to encompass the first and second words of the "Apple Watch" text. These ranges are then used when adding color attributes to the string.

When the example is now run, the words displayed on the label will be rendered in green and red.

20.4 **Using System Fonts**

The system fonts use the same Apple San Francisco font family as the text style font options outlined earlier in this chapter. Unlike text styles, however, system fonts allow attributes such as point size and style (italic, bold etc) to be selected. System font sizes, however, are not subject to the prevailing preferred content size category setting and should be used only when the required results cannot be achieved using text style fonts.

As with text style fonts, system fonts may be selected at design-time within Interface Builder, or specified dynamically in the code of an interface controller.

To select a system font in Interface Builder, select the interface object to which the font is to be applied, display the Attributes Inspector and click on the "T" button in the Font setting field. From the drop-down menu, click on the Font menu button and select either the *System* or *System Italic* option from the options listed under the *System* heading as shown in Figure 20-4:

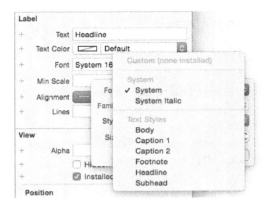

Figure 20-4

Once a system font setting has been selected, a variety of options are available to configure the size and appearance of the font when used to render text. In Figure 20-5, for example, the range of style selections is displayed in the Attribute Inspector font menu:

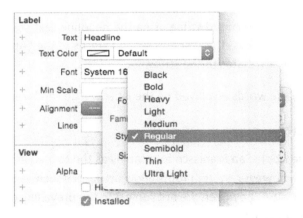

Figure 20-5

As with text style fonts, system font objects can be obtained by making calls to methods of the UIFont class, specifying as a parameter the required point size of the font. Among the system font methods supported by the UIFont class are methods to obtain regular, bold and italic font objects of a specified point size:

```
// Returns a regular 12 pt system font
let regularFont = UIFont.systemFontOfSize(12)

// Returns an italic 14 pt system font
let italicFont = UIFont.italicSystemFontOfSize(14)

// Returns a bold 16 pt system font
```

```
let boldFont = UIFont.boldSystemFontOfSize(16)
```

As with text style fonts, a system font object can be used when rendering text within a WatchKit app scene through the use of attributed strings.

20.5 Summary

WatchKit provides support for text style, system and custom fonts. Text style fonts are referenced by style (body, headline, sub-heading etc.) and are tailored automatically by the UIFont class to match the user's preferred content size category setting.

System fonts, on the other hand, use the same font family as text style fonts but allow the selection of style and point size attributes. System fonts are not subject to the user's preferred content size setting and, as such, should be used only when the desired results cannot be achieved using text styles.

When using fonts in WatchKit app code, it is necessary to use attributed strings to incorporate the font in the text string being displayed. The use of mutable attributed strings allows multiple attributes such as fonts and colors to be included in a single string.

21. A WatchKit App Custom Font Tutorial

WatchKit provides a set of built-in "system" fonts available for use when displaying text within a WatchKit app. In addition to these system fonts it is also possible to install and use custom fonts within a WatchKit app user interface. This chapter will present the steps involved in installing and using a custom font within a WatchKit app project.

21.1 Using Custom Fonts in WatchKit

The system fonts supported by WatchKit can be selected at design time from the Font menu (Figure 21-1) which can be found in the Attributes Inspector when an interface object containing text is selected in a storyboard scene.

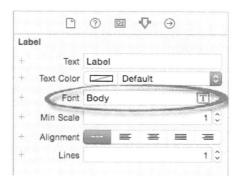

Figure 21-1

When custom fonts are bundled with the project they can be applied to interface objects by clicking on the "T" icon in the Font field and, in the resulting panel, clicking on the current Font setting and selecting the *Custom* option (Figure 21-2) from the resulting menu. If the *Custom* option is not selectable then custom fonts have yet to be added to the project:

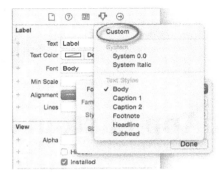

Figure 21-2

Custom fonts may also be applied to text at runtime from within the interface controller class of a scene through the use of *attributed strings*. Custom fonts cannot, however, be used within Notification and Glance scenes.

The remainder of this chapter will work through a tutorial that demonstrates how custom fonts can be added to a WatchKit app project and used both from within Interface Builder and within the code of an interface controller class.

21.2 Downloading a Custom Font

Fonts are supplied in *font files* and can be obtained from a variety of sources at a range of prices and quite often free of charge. WatchKit and iOS currently support TrueType (.ttf) and OpenType (.otf) formats. For the purposes of this example the Sofia font bundled with the sample code archive will be used as the custom font. If you have not already downloaded the sample code for the book it can be obtained from the following URL:

http://www.ebookfrenzy.com/print/watchos2/index.php

Once the package has been downloaded and unpacked, navigate in a Finder window to the *custom_font* folder which contains the *Sofia-Regular.otf* file as outlined in Figure 21-3:

Figure 21-3

This font file will be added to the WatchKit app project later in this chapter so keep the Finder window open.

21.3 Creating the Custom Font Project

Start Xcode and create a new iOS project. On the template screen choose the *Application* option located under *watchOS* in the left hand panel and select *iOS App with WatchKit App*. Click *Next*, set the product name to *CustomFont*, enter your organization identifier and make sure that the *Devices* menu is set to *Universal*. Before clicking *Next*, change the *Language* menu to Swift and switch off all of the *Include* options. On the final screen, choose a location in which to store the project files and click on *Create* to proceed to the main Xcode project window.

21.4 Designing the WatchKit App Scene

Within the Project Navigator panel, locate and select the *Interface.storyboard* file located under the *CustomFont WatchKit App* folder so that it loads into the Interface Builder environment. From the Object Library panel, drag and drop a Group interface object onto the scene canvas. With the Group object selected in the scene, display the Attributes Inspector and change the *Layout* property to *Vertical*. In the Alignment section of the attributes panel change both the *Horizontal* and *Vertical* menus to *Center*.

Drag and drop two Label objects from the Object Library panel onto the Group object in the scene layout. Double-click on the upper label and change the text so it reads "Hello". Shift-click on each Label object so that both are selected and, within the Attributes Inspector panel, change the *Horizontal* Alignment property to *Center*. On completion of these steps, verify that the scene matches the layout shown in Figure 21-4:

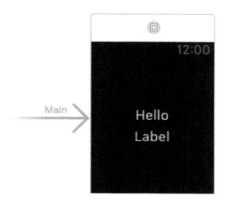

Figure 21-4

The last task to perform within Interface Builder is to establish an outlet connection on the second Label object. Display the Assistant Editor panel, verify that it is displaying the content of the *InterfaceController.swift* file and Ctrl-click and drag from the lower Label to a position immediately beneath the class declaration line in the editor panel. On releasing the line use the connection dialog to establish an outlet named *labelObject*.

21.5 **Adding the Custom Font to the Project**

There are two steps to integrating a custom font into a WatchKit app. The first step is to add the font file to the project. For the purposes of this example, the *Sofia-Regular* font will be used. Locate this font in the Finder window and drag and drop it beneath the *CustomFont WatchKit App* entry in the Xcode project navigator.

Figure 21-5

Since the font will need to be accessible to both the WatchKit App and the extension, make sure that both targets are selected in the options panel (Figure 21-6) before clicking on the *Finish* button:

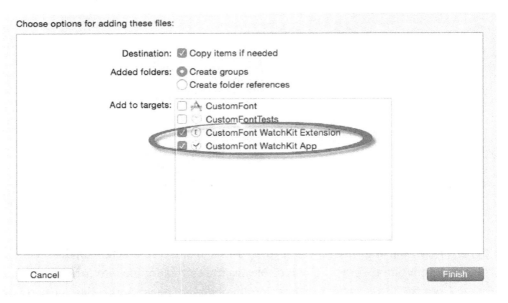

Figure 21-6

In addition to adding the font file to the project and configuring the targets, an entry for the font needs to be added to the *Info.plist* files for both the WatchKit app and extension targets. Begin by selecting the *Info.plist* file located under the *CustomFont WatchKit App* folder in the Project Navigator panel. Once the file has loaded into the property list editor, select the last row in the list so that it highlights in blue. Click on the + button that appears in the selected row to add a new entry to the list. From the dropdown menu that appears, scroll down to and select the *Fonts provided by application* option as illustrated in Figure 21-7:

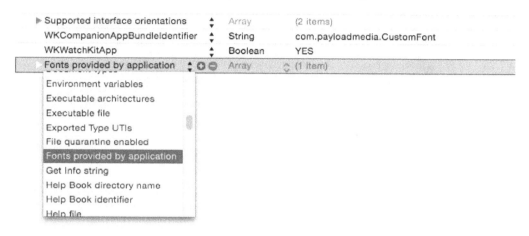

Figure 21-7

Click on the arrow to the left of the newly added row to list the first item in the array of fonts. Double click in the *Value* column of this row to enter into editing mode, type in the full file name of the custom font file including the .otf filename extension and press the keyboard Enter key:

Figure 21-8

The same entry also needs to be added to the *Info.plist* file of the extension target. Select the *Info.plist* file listed under the *CustomFont WatchKit Extension* folder and repeat the above steps to add an entry for the same font file.

With these steps completed it should now be possible to begin using the custom font within the WatchKit app.

21.6 Selecting Custom Fonts in Interface Builder

Once a custom font has been integrated into an Xcode project it should be listed as an option from within the Attributes Inspector panel. To verify this, open the *Interface.storyboard* file, select the upper Label object and display the Attributes Inspector. Click on the "T" icon in the Font field. In the resulting panel, click on the *Font* entry and select *Custom* from the popup menu. With the custom font option selected, the Sofia Regular font should be listed as outlined in Figure 21-9:

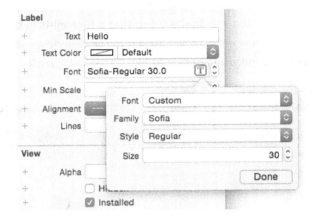

Figure 21-9

Set the *Size* property to 35 points and click on the *Done* button. Refer to the storyboard scene where the "Hello" text should now have been rendered using the custom font selection:

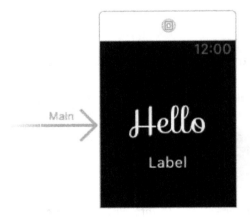

Figure 21-10

21.7 Using Custom Fonts in Code

Custom fonts can also be used in conjunction with attributed string objects to display text at run time from within the interface controller class of a storyboard scene. The technique will now be used to display some text on the second label using the same Sofia custom font.

As previously outlined in the chapter entitled *Working with Fonts and Attributed Strings in WatchKit*, attributed strings are represented using the NSAttributedString and NSMutableAttributedString classes and allow text to be combined with attributes such as fonts and colors. To begin with, a reference to the custom font needs to be obtained. This is achieved using the UIFont class and referencing the font name. Select the *InterfaceController.swift* file and modify the *awakeWithContext* method as follows to create a UIFont object using the custom font:

```
override func awakeWithContext(context: AnyObject?) {
    super.awakeWithContext(context)

    if let customFont = UIFont(name:
            "Sofia-Regular", size: 22) {
    } else {
        print("Font not found")
    }
}
```

The above code attempts to create a font object using the custom Sofia font with a 22pt size and outputs a message in the event that the font could not be found.

The next task is to create a Dictionary object with a key set to *NSFontAttributeName* and the custom font object as the value. This dictionary is then used to specify the attributes for an NSAttributedString instance containing text which reads "Apple Watch". This string is then displayed on the Label object via the previously configured outlet connection:

```
override func awakeWithContext(context: AnyObject?) {
    super.awakeWithContext(context)

    if let customFont = UIFont(name:
            "Sofia-Regular", size: 22) {
        let fontAttributes = [NSFontAttributeName : customFont]

        let attributedText = NSAttributedString(string: "Apple Watch",
            attributes: fontAttributes)

        labelObject.setAttributedText(attributedText)
    } else {
        print("Font not found")
    }
}
```

Compile and run the WatchKit app at which point the second label should display the "Apple Watch" text using the custom font at the designated size:

Figure 21-11

21.8 **Summary**

WatchKit includes a set of system fonts which can be used when displaying text within a WatchKit app scene. Additional fonts may be added to a project as *custom fonts*. This is a process which involves the addition of the font file to the project and the configuration of the Info.plist property files for both the WatchKit app and the extension. Once a custom font has been incorporated into a project it is available both for selection within Interface Builder and as a rendering option from within the code of an interface controller.

When using custom fonts in code, it is necessary to use attributed strings to incorporate the font in the text string being displayed.

22. An Introduction to the WatchKit WKInterfacePicker Object

Traditionally used to wind up or set the time on mechanical watches, Apple has cleverly repurposed the crown on the side of the Apple Watch as an input device. Named the "Digital Crown" the crown on the Apple Watch is used to perform tasks such as scrolling through lists of items and zooming in and out of content.

With the introduction of watchOS 2, the use of the Digital Crown as an input device is now available to WatchKit app developers through the WKInterfacePicker object. This object allows developers to build into WatchKit apps a variety of different features that respond to the Digital Crown.

This chapter will provide an overview of the capabilities of the WKInterfacePicker object before detailed examples are covered in subsequent chapters.

22.1 An Overview of the WKInterfacePicker Object

The WKInterfacePicker object (or picker object) is a versatile class designed specifically for connecting certain types of content displayed within a WatchKit app to the Digital Crown located on the side of the Apple Watch device. The object is primarily intended to present sequences of information to the user and can be configured to present those items using a number of different styles through which the user scrolls by rotating the Digital Crown.

The items presented by the picker object can take the form of text and images in a list format, or even as a sequence of images presented in a stack orientation where the Digital Crown flips from one image to another. Alternatively, images can be presented within the picker as a sequence through which the user smoothly animates back and forth as the crown is turned.

22.2 Adding a Picker Object to a Storyboard Scene

The WKInterfacePicker object is a visual user interface element which is added to a scene simply by dragging and dropping an instance from the Interface Builder Object Library panel onto the scene within the storyboard. Once added, an outlet connection will need to be established within the interface controller class so that the object can be managed from within the code of the WatchKit app. Multiple picker objects can be added to a single scene. When the user selects a picker object by tapping the screen, that picker is said to currently have focus, an indication of which can be shown using an optional outline configuration property.

22.3 Understanding Picker Object Attributes

The look and behavior of a picker object can be configured using a range of attributes which fall into the categories of style, focus and indicator, each of which can be specified from within the Attributes Inspector panel when a picker object is selected within the storyboard scene. Details of these attributes are as follows:

- **Style** – The style attribute dictates the visual appearance of the picker and the way in which the picker items are presented to the user. Each style option will be covered in greater detail in the next section of this chapter.
- **Focus** – The focus attribute dictates the way in which the picker object indicates that it currently has focus within the interface controller scene. A picker object is said to have focus when it is the currently selected item in the scene and is responding to the Digital Crown. Options available for this attribute are for an outline to appear around the picker, for an outline combined with a caption to be visible or for no outline to appear. Figure 22-1, for example, shows a picker object configured with both outline and caption:

Figure 22-1

- **Indicator** – This attribute controls whether or not an indicator is displayed in the top right hand corner of the picker object to provide a visual indication of the user's progress through the list of items presented by the picker.
- **Enabled** – This attribute indicates whether the picker object is able to be selected by the user within the scene.

22.4 Understanding Picker Object Styles

A WKInterfacePicker instance can be configured to present content using one of three different styles:

- **List** – The list style presents the picker items in a vertical stack through which the user scrolls using the Digital Crown. Each item within the list can contain a title, a caption, an accessory image and a content image. The title takes the form of the text that is displayed for the item in the list. If the picker object is configured to display an outline with a caption, the caption property defines the text that is displayed within the outline of the picker. The optional accessory image appears to the left of the title text. The content image, if provided, appears in the background of the list item.

- **Stack** – When configured to use the stack style, the picker items are presented in a form resembling a stack of cards displaying images. At any one time only one item is visible. As the user turns the Digital Crown the current item is animated off the screen and the new one transitioned on screen.
- **Image Sequence** – The image sequence style is ideal for presenting an animated sequence of images whereby the user moves from frame to frame within the animation sequence using the Digital Crown. As outlined in the chapter entitled *A WatchKit WKInterfacePicker Coordinated Animation Example*, multiple animated sequences may be coordinated with the Digital Crown within a single interface controller scene.

22.5 Creating Picker Item Objects

Each item displayed by a picker object is contained within an instance of the WKPickerItem class. When working in List mode, each picker item may be configured with a caption, title, content image and accessory image. For stacked and image sequence modes, only the contentImage property of the WKPickerItem object needs to be set. Images must be provided as WKImage objects.

The WKPickerItem objects are packaged into an array which is passed through to the *setItems* method of the picker object. The following code fragment demonstrates the initialization of a picker object configured to display both title and caption information:

```
var itemList: [(String, String)] = [
    ("Caption 1", "Red"),
    ("Caption 2", "Green"),
    ("Caption 3", "Blue")]

let pickerItems: [WKPickerItem] = itemList.map {
    let pickerItem = WKPickerItem()
    pickerItem.caption = $0.0
    pickerItem.title = $0.1
    return pickerItem
}

myPicker.setItems(pickerItems)
```

The following code, on the other hand is intended for use with a picker configured to use the stack or image sequence styles and populates the picker with a sequence of images contained within the WatchKit app bundle where the image filenames are numbered sequentially using the format my_image<n>@2x.png:

```
var pickerItems = [WKPickerItem]()
```

```
for index in 0...10 {
    let pickerItem = WKPickerItem()
    pickerItem.contentImage = WKImage(imageName: "my_image\(index)")
    pickerItems.append(pickerItem)
}

myPicker.setItems(pickerItems)
```

22.6 Setting the Currently Selected Item

The currently selected picker item may be set programmatically using the *setSelectedItemIndex* method of the picker object passing through an Int value representing the item to be selected:

```
myPicker.setSelectedItemIndex(4)
```

22.7 Coordinating Animations

The animation within a picker object may be coordinated with other animations within the same scene using the *setCoordinatedAnimations* method of the picker object. The other animations within the scene can take the form of animated WKInterfaceImage objects or animations assigned to WKInterfaceGroup objects. The topic of coordinated animations is covered in greater detail in the chapter entitled *A WatchKit WKInterfacePicker Coordinated Animation Example*.

22.8 Requesting Focus for the Picker Object

A call to the *focusForCrownInput* method of a picker object will cause that object to gain focus within the scene in which it is embedded and begin receiving input from the Digital Crown:

```
myPicker.focusForCrownInput()
```

22.9 Enabling and Disabling a Picker Object

In addition to configuring the enabled status of a picker object within the Interface Builder environment at design time, this state may also be configured programmatically by calling the picker object's *setEnabled* method. The following code, for example, disables the referenced picker object:

```
myPicker.setEnabled(false)
```

22.10 Responding to Picker Changes

When the user scrolls from one item to another within a picker object, an event is triggered which, if connected to an action method will result in a call to that method. This action connection can be established within Interface Builder by displaying the Assistant Editor panel and Ctrl-clicking and dragging from the picker object in the storyboard scene to a suitable location in the interface controller class file and establishing an action connection. Once connected, the method will be called each time the user changes the current selection and passed a value indicating the index of the current selection in the array of picker items.

22.11 Summary

The WKInterfacePicker class provides a way for developers to design WatchKit app behavior which responds to input from the Digital Crown control located on the side of the Apple Watch device. The picker object allows content to be presented in a number of different styles and navigated and selected using the Digital Crown. Content can be presented in list form including text and images or as a series of stacked images. Alternatively, content may also be presented in the form of an animation sequence.

Having covered the basics of the WKInterfacePicker class, the next two chapters (*A WatchKit Picker Tutorial* and *A WatchKit WKInterfacePicker Coordinated Animation Example*) will work through examples of practical implementations of the picker object.

23. A WatchKit Picker Tutorial

As outlined in the chapter entitled *An Introduction to the WatchKit WKInterfacePicker Object*, the WKInterfacePicker object can be configured to use a variety of different styles. Having covered the basics of the WKInterfacePicker object in the preceding chapter, this chapter will work through the creation of a project that makes use of the picker object using the List style within a WatchKit app.

The project created in this chapter will consist of color names through which the user is able to scroll using the Digital Crown. As the user scrolls, a Label object will update to display the current item in the list.

23.1 Creating the Picker Project

Start Xcode and create a new iOS project. On the template screen choose the *Application* option located under *watchOS* in the left hand panel and select *iOS App with WatchKit App*. Click *Next*, set the product name to *PickerListApp*, enter your organization identifier and make sure that the *Devices* menu is set to *Universal*. Before clicking *Next*, change the *Language* menu to Swift and switch off all of the *Include* options. On the final screen, choose a location in which to store the project files and click on *Create* to proceed to the main Xcode project window.

23.2 Designing the WatchKit App Scene

Locate and select the *Interface.storyboard* file listed under *PickerListApp WatchKit App* in the Project Navigator panel. Once loaded into Interface Builder, drag and drop a Picker object from the Object Library panel onto the main storyboard scene. Next, drag a Label object and position it immediately beneath the Picker object as illustrated in Figure 23-1. Once the Label has been added, use the Attributes Inspector panel to set the Alignment property in the Label section of the panel to center the text. In the Alignment section, set the Horizontal property to *Center*.

Display the Assistant Editor panel and create outlet connections from the Picker and Label objects named *myPicker* and *itemLabel* respectively.

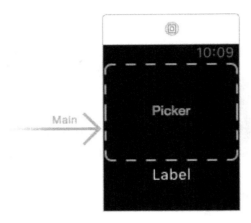

Figure 23-1

Finally, select the Picker object in the scene and, in the Attributes Inspector panel, set the *Style* property to *List* and the *Focus Style* to *Outline with Caption* as shown in Figure 23-2:

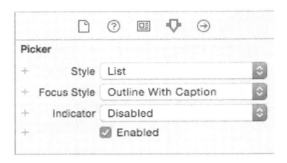

Figure 23-2

23.3 Implementing the Picker List Items

Each picker item will need to have a caption and a title property. The values for these items will be stored in an array of string pairs within the interface controller class. Select the *InterfaceController.swift* file and add this array as follows:

```swift
import WatchKit
import Foundation

class InterfaceController: WKInterfaceController {

    @IBOutlet var myPicker: WKInterfacePicker!
    @IBOutlet var itemLabel: WKInterfaceLabel!

    var itemList: [(String, String)] = [
```

```
            ("Item 1", "Red"),
            ("Item 2", "Green"),
            ("Item 3", "Blue"),
            ("Item 4", "Yellow"),
            ("Item 5", "Indigo"),
            ("Item 6", "Violet") ]

    override func awakeWithContext(context: AnyObject?) {
        super.awakeWithContext(context)

        // Configure interface objects here.
    }
    .
    .
    .
}
```

The code to populate the picker object with the items now needs to be added to the *awakeWithContext* method as follows:

```
override func awakeWithContext(context: AnyObject?) {
    super.awakeWithContext(context)

    let pickerItems: [WKPickerItem] = itemList.map {
        let pickerItem = WKPickerItem()
        pickerItem.caption = $0.0
        pickerItem.title = $0.1
        return pickerItem
    }
    myPicker.setItems(pickerItems)
}
```

The code added to the method works through the items in the array and creates a WKPickerItem object for each one assigning the string values in each array element to the picker item caption and title properties. After each WKPickerItem object has been created and initialized it is added to the array of picker items. Once the array is complete it is passed through to the myPicker object via the *setItems* method.

Compile and run the PickerListApp WatchKit App target and, once running, scroll through the list items using the Digital Crown or, in the case of the Watch Simulator, the mouse scroll wheel:

Figure 23-3

Note that the picker has a green outline as configured and that the caption changes along with the item as the list scrolls.

23.4 Implementing the Action Method

In order to be able to update the Label object with the current selection in the picker list, an action outlet needs to be added to the project. With the Assistant Editor panel displayed, establish an action connection from the picker object to a method named *pickerChanged*. Once the action method has been established, modify the code so that it reads as follows:

```
@IBAction func pickerChanged(value: Int) {
    itemLabel.setText(itemList[value].1)
}
```

The single line of code added to this method takes the value argument passed to the method and uses it as an index into the array of picker items. The color name is then extracted from the array element and set as the text on the Label object in the scene.

23.5 Testing the App

Compile and run the WatchKit app once more and, using either the Digital Crown on a physical Apple Watch device, or the scroll wheel if using the Simulator, verify that the Label object updates as the current item in the picker object changes as illustrated in Figure 23-4:

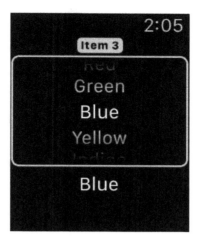

Figure 23-4

23.6 **Summary**

The WKInterfacePicker object in List style mode allows a list of items to be displayed through which the user is able to scroll using the Digital Crown. As the user scrolls through the items in the list, an action method (if implemented) is called and passed the index value of the current list item selection. This chapter has worked through the creation of a project designed to outline the steps in implementing this behavior.

24. A WatchKit WKInterfacePicker Coordinated Animation Example

The WKInterfacePicker object is capable of displaying sequences of images, the animation of which the user controls using the Apple Watch Digital Crown control. As outlined in the chapter entitled *An Introduction to the WatchKit WKInterfacePicker Object*, the picker object may also be used to coordinate the animation of multiple image sequences by associating a WKInterfacePicker object with WKInterfaceGroup or WKInterfaceImage objects within a storyboard scene. The purpose of this chapter is to demonstrate both how the image sequence style of the picker object is implemented within a WatchKit app, and also the steps involved in creating coordinated image animation tied to the Digital Crown.

24.1 About the Coordinated Image Picker Project

When completed, the main scene in the WatchKit app will consist of a sequence of images displaying a percentage value. The percentage value will be surrounded by a progress circle which is animated in coordination with the picker sequence as shown in Figure 24-1:

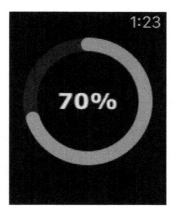

Figure 24-1

When the project is completed and the user turns the Digital Crown both the percentage value and the circle will update accordingly. In practice, the percentage value will be represented by a picker object in image sequence mode and the circle will be an animated image assigned to the background property of a WKInterfaceGroup object in which the picker object is contained.

24.2 Generating Radial Animations

A common use for the picker object in image sequence mode is to display radial progress animations as shown in Figure 24-1. A particularly useful tool for generating radial animations (and the one used to generate the radial image sequence in this example) is Hitesh Maidasani's *Radial Bar Generator for Apple Watch* which is accessible online at:

http://hmaidasani.github.io/RadialChartImageGenerator/

24.3 Creating the Example Project

Start Xcode and create a new iOS project. On the template screen choose the *Application* option located under *watchOS* in the left hand panel and select *iOS App with WatchKit App*. Click *Next*, set the product name to *PickerImagesApp*, enter your organization identifier and make sure that the *Devices* menu is set to *Universal*. Before clicking *Next*, change the *Language* menu to Swift and switch off all of the *Include* options. On the final screen, choose a location in which to store the project files and click on *Create* to proceed to the main Xcode project window.

24.4 Designing the WatchKit App User Interface

Locate and select the *Interface.storyboard* file listed under *PickerImagesApp WatchKit App* in the Project Navigator panel. Once loaded into Interface Builder, drag and drop a Group object from the Object Library panel onto the main storyboard scene. Display the Assistant Editor and establish an outlet connection from the Group object named *myGroup*.

Display the Attributes Inspector panel and change both the *Horizontal* and *Vertical* Alignment settings to *Center*. With the Group object still selected, change the *Height* and *Width* Size properties on the Group object to be *Fixed* at 100:

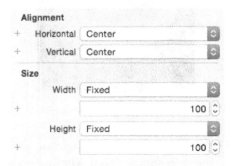

Figure 24-2

Locate the Picker object in the Object Library panel and drag and drop an instance onto the Group object within the storyboard scene. Once again using the Assistant Editor panel, establish an outlet connection from the Picker object named *myPicker*.

With the Picker object still selected in the storyboard scene, change the *Style* property in the Attributes Inspector panel to *Sequence* and both the Horizontal and Vertical Alignment properties to *Center*.

Finally, change both the Height and Width Size properties for the Picker object to be *Fixed*, setting the Width property to 65 and the Height property to 32.

On completion of these steps, the layout for the main scene should match that of Figure 24-3:

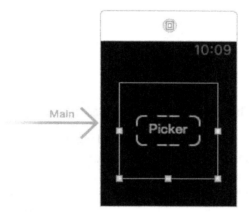

Figure 24-3

24.5 Adding the Picker Image Sequences to the Project

The animation will require two sets of animation sequences, one representing the percentage text and the other the progress circle. The images for the picker object can be found in the sample code download for the book which is available from the following URL:

http://www.ebookfrenzy.com/print/watchos2/index.php

Within the Project Navigator panel, select the *Assets.xcassets* entry listed under *PickerImagesApp WatchKit App* so that the asset catalog loads into the main Xcode panel. Ctrl-click in the center panel beneath the AppIcon entry and, from the resulting menu, select the *Import...* menu option.

In the file selection dialog, navigate to and select the *picker_images* folder in the sample code archive folder and click on the *Open* button. All of the images needed for the percentage animation sequence will now be added to the asset catalog of the WatchKit app bundle:

A WatchKit WKInterfacePicker Coordinated Animation Example

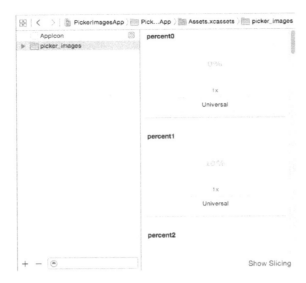

Figure 24-4

24.6 Adding the Group Background Image Sequences to the Project

The images for the Group object background are contained within the *group_images* folder of the sample code download and must be added to the asset catalog of the WatchKit app extension.

Within the Project Navigator panel, select the *Assets.xcassets* entry listed under *PickerImagesApp WatchKit Extension* so that the asset catalog loads into the main Xcode panel. Ctrl-click in the center panel and, from the resulting menu, select the *Import...* menu option.

In the file selection dialog, navigate to and select the *group_images* folder in the sample code folder and click on the *Open* button. All of the images needed for the radial animation sequence will now be added to the asset catalog of the WatchKit extension.

24.7 Implementing the Picker Animation Sequence

With the scene layout designed and both sets of animation images added to the project the next step is to initialize the Picker object with the sequence of images. The images for the picker object are named *percent<n>@2x.png* where n is numbered from 0 to 10. The code for the interface controller needs to create an array of WKPickerItems to be passed to the picker object. Each WKPickerItem object needs to have assigned to the *contentImage* property a WKImage object initialized with one of the sequence image files. Once the array of items has been created it then needs to be assigned to the picker object.

The code to achieve this can now be added to the *awakeWithContext* method located in the *InterfaceController.swift* file as follows:

194

```
override func awakeWithContext(context: AnyObject?) {
    super.awakeWithContext(context)

    var pickerItems = [WKPickerItem]()

    for index in 0...10 {
        let pickerItem = WKPickerItem()
        pickerItem.contentImage = WKImage(imageName: "percent\(index)")
        pickerItems.append(pickerItem)
    }
    myPicker.setItems(pickerItems)
}
```

With the code added to the method, compile and run the app and verify that the first image displayed shows 0% and that turning the Digital Crown (or mouse scroll wheel if using the Simulator) animates through the full sequence of images up to 100%.

24.8 Configuring the Group Background Animation

The next step is to create an animated image using the circle image sequence and assign it to the background of the Group object. Once created and assigned to the group object, the animation needs to be coordinated with the picker object via a call to the object's *setCoordinatedAnimations* method. The code to achieve these steps should also be added to the *awakeWithContext* method of the *InterfaceController.swift* file as follows:

```
override func awakeWithContext(context: AnyObject?) {
    super.awakeWithContext(context)

    var pickerItems = [WKPickerItem]()

    for index in 0...10 {
        let pickerItem = WKPickerItem()
        pickerItem.contentImage = WKImage(imageName: "percent\(index)")
        pickerItems.append(pickerItem)
    }
    myPicker.setItems(pickerItems)

    var imageArray = [UIImage]()

    for index in 0...10 {
        let image = UIImage(named: "progressarc\(index)")
        imageArray.append(image!)
    }
```

```
    let progressImages = UIImage.animatedImageWithImages(imageArray,
        duration: 0.0)
myGroup.setBackgroundImage(progressImages)
myPicker.setCoordinatedAnimations([myGroup])
}
```

24.9 **Testing the App**

Compile and run the WatchKit app once again and test that turning the Digital Crown results in the coordinated animation of both image sequences:

Figure 24-5

24.10 **Summary**

In addition to allowing the Digital Crown to control the animation sequence assigned to a single picker object, combining the picker with one or more group or image objects allows multiple animations to be synchronized. This chapter has demonstrated the use of this technique to coordinate the animations of a picker image sequence with the background animation assigned to a group object.

25. Sharing Media Files Using App Groups

It has already been established in previous chapters that both the WatchKit app and WatchKit extension are installed and execute on the Apple Watch device. Regardless of this fact, however, the WatchKit extension and the WatchKit app each run within separate processes. This process separation (sometimes referred to as "sandboxing") means that the WatchKit app and WatchKit extension do not, by default, have access to each other's file storage. While this is not generally a problem, it can become an issue when working with media files.

The responsibility for playing back video content, for example, lies within the WatchKit app. This raises the question of how the WatchKit app would gain access to the video file to be played if it has been downloaded into the container of the WatchKit extension, an area to which the WatchKit app has no access. A similar problem arises when recording audio content. Once again the WatchKit app is responsible for the recording and will, by default, save that to a media file within its own container where the WatchKit extension will be unable to access it. The solution to this problem can be found in app groups.

This chapter will explore the use of app groups to enable a WatchKit extension and the corresponding WatchKit app to share access to files. In a later chapter entitled *Recording and Playing Audio in a WatchKit App* this particular use of app groups will be demonstrated in a practical example.

25.1 Sandboxes, Containers and User Defaults

Although both the containing WatchKit app and the extension for a WatchKit app both execute on the same physical Apple Watch device they are said to run in separate sandbox environments. Sandboxes are a security mechanism that enforce sets of rules in terms of what an app can and cannot do when running on an Apple Watch device. Sandboxing, for example, prevents one app on a device from interfering with, or accessing files and data belonging to another app installed on the same device.

Included within the sandbox of each app is a *container*. This is essentially a file system area containing directories into which the app can store and access files. These can be any type of file including images, videos, plain text files or even SQLite or Core Data databases. The sandbox rules dictate that an app in one sandbox cannot access the files in the container of a second app and these same rules apply equally to the relationship between a WatchKit extension and the corresponding WatchKit app.

25.2 **Sharing Data Using App Groups**

The sharing of files between a WatchKit extension and the WatchKit app can be achieved through the use of shared app groups. When the WatchKit app and WatchKit extension are enrolled in the same app group they are given access to a shared container. This allows files to be shared between the WatchKit app and the extension. The diagram in Figure 25-1 illustrates this concept:

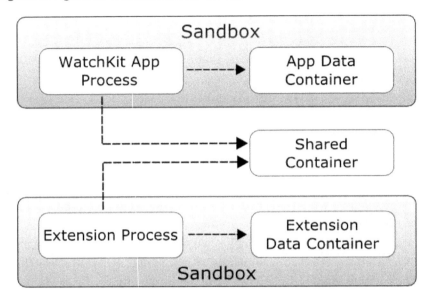

Figure 25-1

25.3 **Adding the WatchKit App and Extension to an App Group**

App Group settings are contained in entitlement files using the *com.apple.security.application-groups* key. Both the WatchKit extension and the WatchKit app must include this entitlement. The value assigned to the *com.apple.security.application-groups* key indicates the app group to which membership is required. This value is typically set to the package name of the app prefixed with "group." and must match in both the WatchKit app and extension entitlement files.

While it is possible to manually create the necessary entitlement files, by far the easiest way to configure app group membership is to do so through the Xcode Capabilities panel. To configure app group support for the WatchKit app, select the target located at the top of the Project Navigator panel and click on the *Capabilities* tab in the main panel. Within the capabilities panel, locate the *App Groups* section and switch it to the *On* position:

Figure 25-2

When app groups have been enabled in the Capabilities screen, any existing app groups associated with your Apple developer account will be listed. To make the current app a member of any of those groups simply enable the checkbox next to the group name:

Figure 25-3

To add a new app group to your account, simply click on the + button and enter the new app group name. Add the current app to the newly added app group by enabling the checkbox next to the group name. The app group will subsequently appear as an option in all other project targets within the Xcode Capabilities panel.

With the WatchKit app added to the app group, the WatchKit extension must also be added as a member of the same group in order to gain access to the shared container. To access the capability settings for the WatchKit Extension, use the menu located in the top left-hand corner of the Capabilities panel as indicated in Figure 25-4:

Figure 25-4

When clicked, this menu will present a list of targets contained within the current project as shown in Figure 25-5, one of which will be the WatchKit extension. Select this option and repeat the steps followed for the WatchKit app to enable and configure app group support, making sure to select the same group name as that chosen for the WatchKit app.

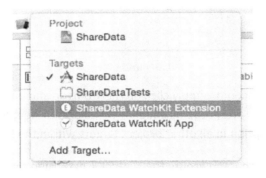

Figure 25-5

A review of the files in the Project Navigator panel will reveal that entitlement files have been added for each of the two targets, the contents of which will read as follows (allowing for differences in the app group name):

```
<?xml version="1.0" encoding="UTF-8"?>
<!DOCTYPE plist PUBLIC "-//Apple//DTD PLIST 1.0//EN"
"http://www.apple.com/DTDs/PropertyList-1.0.dtd">
<plist version="1.0">
<dict>
        <key>com.apple.security.application-groups</key>
        <array>
                <string>group.com.ebookfrenzy.SharingData</string>
        </array>
</dict>
```

```
</plist>
```

With both the parent WatchKit app and the WatchKit extension added to the same app group, code can now be written to access the shared data container.

25.4 **App Group File Sharing**

The first step in terms of sharing files via an app group is to identify the URL of the shared container. This can be achieved by obtaining a reference to the app's default NSFileManager instance and making a call to the *containerURLForSecurityApplicationGroupIdentifier* method of that object, passing through as an argument the name of the app group. For example:

```
let fileManager = NSFileManager.defaultManager()

let url =
    fileManager.containerURLForSecurityApplicationGroupIdentifier(
                        "group.com.ebookfrenzy.SharingData")
```

Once the URL has been obtained, it can be used to share files. When writing data to flat files in a container shared by two processes, Apple advices against using the standard file coordination techniques and recommends using atomic write operations to avoid deadlocks occurring. An atomic write operation writes new data to a temporary file and then renames it to replace the original file. The following code, for example, obtains a reference to the shared container, appends a file name (datafile.dat) to the URL, checks that the file exists and then atomically writes a string to it:

```
let fileManager = NSFileManager.defaultManager()

let url =
    fileManager.containerURLForSecurityApplicationGroupIdentifier(
                "group.com.ebookfrenzy.SharingData")

let dirPath = url?.path
let filePath = dirPath?.stringByAppendingPathComponent("datafile.dat")

if fileManager.fileExistsAtPath(filePath!) {
    let databuffer = ("hello world"
            as NSString).dataUsingEncoding(NSUTF8StringEncoding)
    databuffer?.writeToFile(filePath!, atomically: true)
}
```

25.5 **Summary**

The WatchKit extension and WatchKit app are separate processes that execute within individual sandbox environments. The purpose of sandboxing is to prevent one process from accessing the files and data stored by another process. In order for media files to be shared between the WatchKit app and the WatchKit extension, both must belong to the same app group. App groups allow processes to share files through a shared container.

26. Playing Movies and Audio using the WKInterfaceMovie Class

New in watchOS 2, the WKInterfaceMovie class is a user interface control designed specifically to embed video and audio playback into apps running on the Apple Watch. This chapter will provide an overview of this class before working through the creation of an example WatchKit app.

26.1 An Introduction to WKInterfaceMovie

The WKInterfaceMovie class is a visual object designed to be placed within the storyboard scene of a WatchKit interface controller. Visually, the movie object appears as a rectangular control over which is superimposed a play button as shown in Figure 26-1. When the play button is tapped by the user the media associated with the object is then played.

Figure 26-1

By default, the WKInterfaceMovie object is presented with a black screen area until the user taps the play button. This blank screen may be replaced by an optional *poster* image as illustrated in Figure 26-2:

Figure 26-2

If the user taps the screen at any point while the content is playing the playback is paused. While in this paused state the play button re-appears along with a volume control slider and a progress bar. A *Done* button is also provided to allow the user to return to the interface controller from which playback was originally initiated:

Figure 26-3

26.2 Configuring a WKInterfaceMovie Instance

The WKInterfaceMovie object is included in the Object Library panel within the Xcode Interface Builder tool from where it can be dragged and dropped onto a storyboard scene. Once added to the scene, attributes are available to configure the optional poster image file and the resizing behavior of the content. The resizing options provided are as follows:

- **ResizeAspect** – The content is resized to fit within the bounds of the movie player object while maintaining the aspect ratio of the original movie content. In order to preserve aspect ratio some border areas of the movie player rectangle may remain unfilled in this mode.
- **ResizeAspectFill** – The content is resized to entirely fill the bounds of the movie player object while preserving the aspect ratio of the content. Content that does not fit within the movie player is clipped when using this mode.
- **Resize** – The content is resized to fit the entire movie player bounds without attempting to preserve the aspect ratio of the movie content.

These resizing attributes may be set initially from within the Interface Builder environment, or programmatically at runtime via the object's *setVideoGravity* method. The poster image may also be set from within code using the *setPosterImage* method.

The content to be played may only be specified from within the code of the app and is defined by passing through the content URL to the *setMovieURL* method of the WKInterfaceMovie object. Playback may also be configured to loop repeatedly by passing a *true* value through to the *setLoops* method.

26.3 **Directly Playing Content**

Obviously the WKInterfaceMovie class involves the placement of a user interface object in a storyboard scene which the user must tap in order to initiate audio or video playback. Situations may arise, however, where playback needs to be triggered automatically in response to some other form of event such as a button being tapped or the user selecting a movie clip from a table list. Playback of this kind can be initiated via a call to the *presentMediaPlayerControllerWithURL* method of the WKInterfaceController class. This method displays the same playback interface as that used by the WKInterfaceMovie class but allows playback to auto-play and does not require the placement of a user interface object into the storyboard scene.

The *presentMediaPlayerControllerWithURL* method takes as parameters the URL of the content to be played, a dictionary containing options such as whether playback should start automatically and a completion handler closure containing any necessary code to be executed once playback completes. On completion of playback the completion handler is passed a Boolean value indicating whether or not playback ran to the end of the content, the time into the content at which playback stopped and an NSError object containing details of any errors encountered:

```
let options = [WKMediaPlayerControllerOptionsAutoplayKey : "true"]

presentMediaPlayerControllerWithURL(saveUrl!, options: options, completion:
{ didPlayToEnd, endTime, error in

        // Code here is called after playback ends or fails
})
```

The above example code configures the playback to automatically start. The full range of configuration options when calling this method are as follows:

- **WKMediaPlayerControllerOptionsAutoplayKey** – When set to true playback is initiated automatically once the specified media has loaded.
- **WKMediaPlayerControllerOptionsStartTimeKey** – An NSTimeInterval value indicating the number of seconds into the content at which playback is to start.
- **WKMediaPlayerControllerOptionsVideoGravityKey** – The video gravity setting to be used when playing video content. These values are the same as those previously described for the WKInterfaceMovie class.
- **WKMediaPlayerControllerOptionsLoopsKey** - When set to true this option causes playback to loop continuously.

26.4 **Creating the WKInterfaceMovie Example**

Start Xcode and create a new iOS project. On the template screen choose the *Application* option located under *watchOS* in the left hand panel and select *iOS App with WatchKit App*. Click *Next*, set the product name to *MoviePlayerApp*, enter your organization identifier and make sure that the *Devices* menu is set to *Universal*. Before clicking *Next*, change the *Language* menu to Swift and switch off all of the *Include* options. On the final screen, choose a location in which to store the project files and click on *Create* to proceed to the main Xcode project window.

26.5 **Designing the WatchKit App Scene**

Select the *Interface.storyboard* file located under *MoviePlayerApp WatchKit App* and drag and drop a Movie object from the Object Library onto the scene within the storyboard so that the scene matches that shown in Figure 26-4:

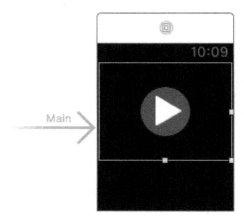

Figure 26-4

The poster image used in the example can be found in the *video_files* folder of the sample code download available from the following URL:

http://www.ebookfrenzy.com/print/watchos2/index.php

Locate and select the *Assets.xcassets* file located under the *MoviePlayerApp WatchKit App* entry in the Project Navigator panel and drag and drop the *movie_poster@2x.png* file from the *video_files* folder of the sample code folder onto the left hand panel of the asset catalog as illustrated in Figure 26-5:

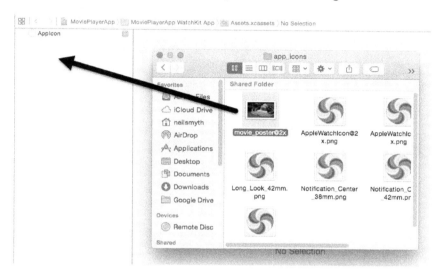

Figure 26-5

Select the *Interface.storyboard* file once again, display the Attributes Inspector panel and select the Movie object within the main scene. Using the menus in the Attributes Inspector panel, set the *Video Gravity* property to *Resize Aspect* and select the *movie_poster* asset from the *Poster Image* menu:

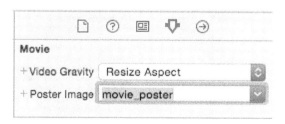

Figure 26-6

Finally, display the Assistant Editor and establish an outlet connection from the Movie object to the *InterfaceController.swift* file named *moviePlayer*.

26.6 **Adding the Video File to the Project**

The video file used in this project is named *movieclip.mov* and is included in the *video_files* folder of the sample code download. Locate this file and drag and drop it beneath the *MoviePlayerApp WatchKit Extension* entry in the Project Navigator panel (Figure 26-7):

Figure 26-7

26.7 **Configuring the Movie URL**

All that remains before testing the app is to assign the URL for the movie clip to the WKInterfaceMovie object in the interface controller scene. To achieve this task, select the *InterfaceController.swift* file and modify the *awakeWithContext* method so that it obtains the URL of the video file from the app bundle and assigns it to the movie object:

```
override func awakeWithContext(context: AnyObject?) {
    super.awakeWithContext(context)

    let url = NSBundle.mainBundle().URLForResource("movieclip",
            withExtension: "mov")

    moviePlayer.setMovieURL(url!)
}
```

26.8 **Testing the App**

Compile and run the WatchKit app either on a physical Apple Watch device or using the simulator and, once running, tap the play button that appears over the top of the poster image in the user interface. Once tapped, the movie player screen should appear and begin playback of the movie clip. If a Bluetooth headset is connected the audio will play through the headset. If no headset is present the audio will be directed to the built-in speakers of the Apple Watch.

26.9 Summary

The WKInterfaceMovie class was introduced as part of the WatchKit SDK for watchOS 2. This new class provides the ability to play movie or audio content to the user from within an Apple Watch app. This chapter has provided an overview of the capabilities of the WKInterfaceController class and worked through the creation of a simple WatchKit app designed to play a short movie clip on the Apple Watch device.

27. Recording and Playing Audio in a WatchKit App

Another new feature introduced into watchOS 2 is the ability to record audio via the Apple Watch device. This involves the use of the audio recording controller which can be configured with a variety of options including audio recording quality and the maximum duration of the recording session.

This chapter will introduce the audio recording controller and implement an example audio recording and playback WatchKit app.

27.1 The Audio Recording Controller

The audio recording controller is launched using a call to the *presentAudioRecorderControllerWithOutputURL* method of the WKInterfaceController class and, when launched, presents the user with the user interface shown in Figure 27-1:

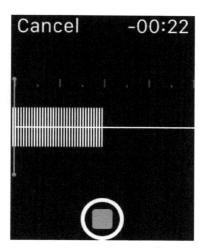

Figure 27-1

To start recording, the user simply taps the red record button and then is able to monitor the recording level using the graph. If a maximum recording duration has been specified, a countdown time appears in the top right hand corner of the scene. Recording is stopped when the specified duration is reached, by tapping the record button a second time, or cancelled entirely using the Cancel button in the upper left hand corner.

Once the recording has been stopped (as opposed to cancelled) the display changes to provide the user with the option of playing back the recorded audio (Figure 27-2). Options are also provided to cancel the recorded audio without saving, or to save the audio. The text displayed on the save button is configured via an option passed through to the *presentAudioRecorderControllerWithOutputURL* method. By default, this button displays text which reads "Save".

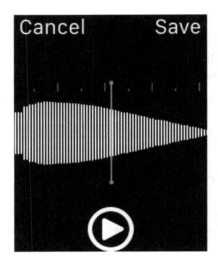

Figure 27-2

If the user selects the save button the audio is saved to the file referenced by the URL passed to the method call. If the URL references a .wav file the audio is saved in LPCM format. If any other file extension is used, the audio will be saved in ACC format.

27.2 Launching the Audio Recording Controller

The audio recording controller is launched via a call to the *presentAudioRecordingControllerWithURL* method of the current interface controller instance. This method expects the following parameters when called:

- A URL referencing the audio file into which the recorded content is to be saved.
- An audio recording quality preset value.
- A dictionary object containing options such as the duration of the recording, the title to be displayed on the action button and whether or not the recording should start automatically.
- A completion handler to be called when recording is complete.

The following code, for example, configures recording for 10 seconds using the narrow band speech quality preset with the save button text set to "Store":

```
let duration = NSTimeInterval(10)

let recordOptions =
    [WKAudioRecorderControllerOptionsMaximumDurationKey : duration,
     WKAudioRecorderControllerOptionsActionTitleKey: "Store"]
presentAudioRecorderControllerWithOutputURL(saveUrl!,
    preset: .NarrowBandSpeech,
    options: recordOptions as [NSObject : AnyObject],
    completion: { saved, error in
            // Completion handler code here
})
```

On completion of the recording session, the completion handler is called and passed a Boolean value indicating whether or not the user chose to save the recording and an NSError object.

The recording controller supports three audio recording quality presets:

- **WKAudioRecordingPreset.NarrowBandSpeech** – Recommended for voice recording, this preset uses an 8kHz sampling rate formatted using LPCM or ACC at 128 kbps.
- **WKAudioRecordingPreset.WideBandSpeech** – Recommended for higher quality speech recording this preset uses a 16kHz sampling rate formatted using LPCM 256 kbps or ACC 24 kbps.
- **WKAudioRecordingPreset.HighQualityAudio** – The highest quality recording preset, this option uses a 44.1kHz sampling rate formatted using LPCM 705.6 kbps or ACC 96 kbps.

Given the inherent storage capacity restriction of the Apple Watch, the lowest acceptable audio quality preset should be used wherever possible to conserve space.

The full range option keys available to configure the audio recording session are as follows:

- **WKAudioRecorderControllerOptionsMaximumDurationKey** – Specifies the maximum permitted duration of the recording session.
- **WKAudioRecorderControllerOptionsActionTitleKey** – The text to be displayed on the action button located in the top right hand corner of the audio recorder controller scene.
- **WKAudioRecorderControllerOptionsAlwaysShowActionTitleKey** – A Boolean value indicating whether or not the action button is displayed within the controller.
- **WKAudioRecorderControllerOptionsAutorecordKey** – A Boolean value controlling whether or not the recording starts automatically when the controller is presented to the user.

27.3 **Using App Groups to Share Media File Access**

As discussed in the *Sharing Data Between a WatchKit App and the WatchKit Extension* chapter, it is important when working with media files to be aware that those files need to be accessible to both the WatchKit app and the corresponding WatchKit extension. When recording audio, the WatchKit app is responsible for storing the recorded audio to file. In terms of playing back the audio, however, the extension will need to be able to reference the saved audio file. When recording or playing back audio, therefore, it is important that an app group shared container be used for the storage of the recorded audio.

27.4 **The Audio Recording and Playback Tutorial**

The remainder of this chapter will work through the creation of a simple WatchKit app designed to record, save and playback audio content using the Apple Watch as both the playback and recording device.

Start Xcode and create a new iOS project. On the template screen choose the *Application* option located under *watchOS* in the left hand panel and select *iOS App with WatchKit App.* Click *Next,* set the product name to *RecordApp,* enter your organization identifier and make sure that the *Devices* menu is set to *Universal.* Before clicking *Next*, change the *Language* menu to Swift and switch off all of the *Include* options. On the final screen, choose a location in which to store the project files and click on *Create* to proceed to the main Xcode project window

27.5 **Designing the Main Storyboard Scene**

Within the Project Navigator panel select the *Interface.storyboard* file located under the *RecordApp WatchKit App* entry. Within Interface Builder, add two Button objects to the main scene and change the text on the buttons to read "Play" and "Record" respectively:

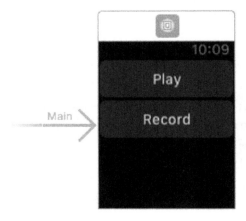

Figure 27-3

Select the Play button, display the Attributes Inspector and switch off the *enabled* property. The button will only be enabled after a recording has been saved.

Display the Assistant Editor and establish an outlet connection from the Play button named *playButton.* With the Assistant Editor still displayed, establish action connections from the Play and Record buttons to methods named *playAudio* and *recordAudio* respectively.

27.6 Creating and Joining the App Group

An app group container will be used to share the media file containing the recorded audio between the WatchKit app and the WatchKit extension. Begin by selecting the RecordApp target located at the top of the Project Navigator panel and, in the Settings panel, select the *Capabilities* tab and click on the target menu located in the top left hand corner of the panel (highlighted in Figure 27-4):

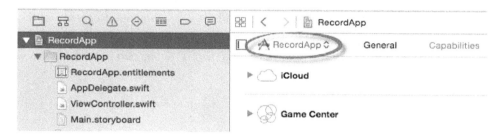

Figure 27-4

From the target menu (Figure 27-5) select the *RecordApp WatchKit App* target:

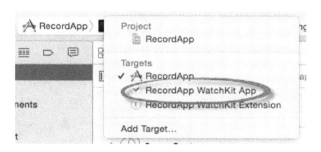

Figure 27-5

Remaining on the Capabilities screen, enable App Groups. When app groups have been enabled, any existing app groups associated with your Apple developer account will be listed.

To add a new app group to your account, simply click on the + button and enter the new app group name, for example:

```
group.com.example.RecordApp
```

Add the current app to the newly added app group by enabling the checkbox next to the group name.

With the WatchKit app added to the app group, the WatchKit extension must also be added as a member of the same group in order to gain access to the shared container. To access the capability settings for the WatchKit extension, use the menu located in the top left-hand corner of the Capabilities panel as indicated in Figure 27-4.

When clicked, this menu will once again present a list of targets contained within the current project, one of which will be the *RecordApp WatchKit Extension*. Select this option, enable App Group support and select the same app group as that configured for the WatchKit app.

27.7 Constructing the Save File URL

If the user chooses to save a recording the file will be saved to the app group shared container. For the purposes of this example, the audio will be saved in a file named *audiofile.wav*. The code to construct this location now needs to be added to the *awakeWithContext* method of the *InterfaceController.swift* file as follows where <YOUR APP GROUP HERE> is replaced by the name assigned to your app group in the previous section:

```
import WatchKit
import Foundation

class InterfaceController: WKInterfaceController {

    var saveUrl: NSURL?

    @IBOutlet var playButton: WKInterfaceButton!

    override func awakeWithContext(context: AnyObject?) {
        super.awakeWithContext(context)

        let fileManager = NSFileManager.defaultManager()

        let container =
    fileManager.containerURLForSecurityApplicationGroupIdentifier(
            "<YOUR APP GROUP HERE>")

        let fileName = "audioFile.wav"

        saveUrl = container?.URLByAppendingPathComponent(fileName)
    }
    .
    .
    .
}
```

27.8 **Implementing the Recording Code**

The code to launch the audio recording controller now needs to be added to the *recordAudio* action method. Select the *InterfaceController.swift* file, locate this method and implement the code as follows:

```
@IBAction func recordAudio() {

    let duration = NSTimeInterval(10)

    let recordOptions =
        [WKAudioRecorderControllerOptionsMaximumDurationKey : duration]

    presentAudioRecorderControllerWithOutputURL(saveUrl!,
        preset: .NarrowBandSpeech,
        options: recordOptions,
        completion: { saved, error in

            if let err = error {
                print(err.description)
            }

            if saved {
                self.playButton.setEnabled(true)
            }
    })
}
```

The code begins by disabling the Play button and then configures a constant to represent a duration of 10 seconds and adds it to an options dictionary. The audio recording controller is then displayed using the URL created in the *awakeWithContext* method, the options dictionary and the narrow band speech preset. Finally, the Play button is enabled if the user saved the audio content.

27.9 **Implementing the Playback Code**

The final task is to implement the code in the *playAudio* method to play back the recorded content. Remaining in the *InterfaceController.swift* file, locate this method and modify it as follows:

```
@IBAction func playAudio() {

    let options = [WKMediaPlayerControllerOptionsAutoplayKey : "true"]

    presentMediaPlayerControllerWithURL(saveUrl!, options: options,
            completion: { didPlayToEnd, endTime, error in
```

```
                    if let err = error {
                            print(err.description)
                    }
        })
}
```

The code added to the method uses the *presentMediaPlayerControllerWithURL* method as described in the previous chapter (*Playing Movies and Audio using the WKInterfaceMovie Class*) to play back the recorded audio file.

27.10 Testing the WatchKit App

Compile and run the WatchKit app on either a physical Apple Watch device or a Simulator session. Record some audio and then use the Play button to play it back. Note that when running on a physical Apple Watch device a request may appear on the paired iPhone seeking permission for the app to use the microphone.

27.11 Summary

Along with the introduction of watchOS 2 came the ability to record and playback audio via the Apple Watch device. Recording of audio involves the use of the audio recording controller which presents the user with the controls necessary to record and save audio via the Apple Watch microphone. Options are provided which allow the WatchKit app to designate both the quality of recording and the maximum duration permitted for the session.

28. An Overview of ClockKit and Apple Watch Complications

With all of the excitement surrounding the Apple Watch and the wonderful things it can do it is easy to lose sight of the fact that most of the instances when a user looks at the device on their wrist they will be doing so simply to check the time of day. In recognition of this fact, Apple has added the ability for WatchKit app developers to embed information into the clock faces presented on the Apple Watch when the user checks the time. These small fragments of information are referred to as Complications and are the topic of this chapter.

28.1 What is a Complication?

A complication is a small fragment of information relating to a timeline provided by a WatchKit app which is displayed alongside the time and date in the clock faces of an Apple Watch. A calendar app might, for example, use a complication so that the user can see the date and time of the next upcoming appointment simply by glancing at the clock face in which the complication has been enabled.

The watchOS system includes a number of different clock faces ranging from Mickey Mouse to a standard clock face, each of which supports a variety of different complications. Figure 28-1, for example, highlights the complications available within the Apple Watch Modular clock face:

Figure 28-1

In actual fact, with the exception of the current time of day, every other piece of information presented in the clock face in Figure 28-1 is provided by a complication.

In addition to seeing the next pending event, the user is also able to use a "Time Travel" feature to scroll backwards and forwards through the timelines of the displayed complications simply by turning the Digital Crown to display past and future timeline events:

Figure 28-2

The complications that are embedded into a particular clock face are selected by the user by performing a force touch "deep press" on the clock face, tapping the *Customize* button and sliding to the complication customization screen, an example of which is illustrated in Figure 28-3:

Figure 28-3

A number of different complications are included with watchOS such as calendar appointments, temperature, moon phase and weather information. With the introduction of watchOS 2 and the ClockKit framework, it is now possible for developers to also provide complications for WatchKit apps.

28.2 Complication Families and Templates

Clearly complications come in different shapes and sizes depending on the clock face and the location of the complication in the face. The size and location of each complication is dictated entirely by watchOS and each complication provided by a WatchKit app must conform to a complication family template. There are currently five complication templates available for selection when developing a complication and these are illustrated in Figure 28-4:

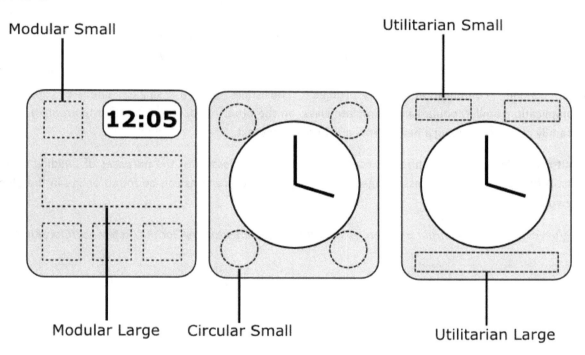

Figure 28-4

When implementing complications Apple recommends that as many complication families as possible be supported by the WatchKit app. This increases the chances that a complication for your app will be available for the user's preferred clock face.

28.3 The Complication Data Source

In order to be able to provide complication support, a WatchKit app must designate a class to act as the complication data source. This class must implement the CLKComplicationDataSource protocol and contain a range of methods which will be called by the ClockKit framework to obtain timeline entries to be displayed on the clock face. When timeline entries are requested from the data source, these entries will need to be returned in the form of CLKComplicationTimeLineEntry objects.

28.4 Complication Timeline Entry Objects

Timeline entry objects are returned by the complication data source of your WatchKit app and contain the date at which the entry is to be displayed together with a template object containing the text and image information to be displayed within the complication.

28.5 Complication Template Objects

Each timeline entry object must contain a complication template object which contains the content to be displayed to the user within the complication. A wide range of template classes (all of which are subclassed from the CLKComplicationTemplate class) is available for use depending on the complication family and the combination of images and text that is to be displayed within a complication. The CLKComplicationTemplateModularSmallSimpleText template class, for example, would be used to create a modular small complication family object consisting of a single line of text. The CLKComplicationFamilyModularLarge template class, on the other hand, would be used to create a modular large family object containing a header row and two lines of text.

ClockKit currently provides 22 different complication template classes for the purposes of building template objects. A full listing of these classes together with detailed descriptions can be found online in the ClockKit Framework Reference:

https://developer.apple.com/library/prerelease/watchos/documentation/ClockKit/Reference/ClockKit_frame work

Once a template object has been created, the next step is to add the content that is to be displayed. This is achieved using text and image provider classes.

28.6 Text Provider Classes

Once an appropriate template object has been created it needs to be populated with the content to be displayed in the form of text and images. Instead of using UIImage and String objects to provide this content, however, complication content is constructed using text and image providers.

Text providers are derived from the CLKTextProvider class and provide a variety of options for providing text to be displayed in a complication. The advantage of using text providers is that they can automatically adjust the text to make the best use of the available space within the complication.

The text providers supported in watchOS 2 can be summarized as follows:

- **CLKDateTextProvider** – Automatically formats date information so that it best fits into the available complication space.
- **CLKRelativeDateTextProvider** – Automatically formats text representing the difference in time between the current date and a specified date.
- **CLKSimpleTextProvider** – Allows a line of text to be specified in both long and abbreviated forms. On smaller complications, the abbreviated form will be used.
- **CLKTimeIntervalTextProvider** – Used to convey a range of time (for example 9:00am – 10:30am) automatically configured to make the best use of the available space within a complication.
- **CLKTimeTextProvider** – Used to convey a single time value which is automatically configured to match the available space.

28.7 Image Provider Class

Images are added to timeline objects using the CLKImageProvider class. This class is passed image and optional tint values. Images can be constructed from a foreground image, or by passing through both background and foreground images which are superimposed to create a single image.

When the user customizes a clock face the option is provided to change the tint color of the face. This tint setting is also applied to both the images and text contained within the complications visible in the clock face. As such, any images included in a complication must be provided as *alpha template* images. This means that the image must contain only the alpha channel (which controls the level of transparency of the image) and no RGB (red, green and blue) color channel information. This allows ClockKit to adjust the tint of the image to match the user's color preferences. When creating an image using both background and foreground images, the background image is tinted while the foreground remains in black or white.

28.8 Creating a Timeline Entry Object

Having explored the various elements that comprise a complication timeline entry object, now is a good time to look at what the code to create such an object might look like. The following code, for example, creates a new timeline object:

```
let template = CLKComplicationTemplateModularLargeStandardBody()
let myImage = UIImage(named: "my_image")

template.headerImageProvider = CLKImageProvider(onePieceImage: myImage!)

template.headerTextProvider =
            CLKSimpleTextProvider(text: "11:30 Sales Meeting")
template.body1TextProvider =
            CLKSimpleTextProvider(text: "Conference Rm 1 Building 2")
```

```
let entry = CLKComplicationTimelineEntry(date: NSDate(),
            complicationTemplate: template)
```

The above code creates a new modular large standard body template object and creates an image object using an image asset name "my_image". An image provider is then created using the image object and assigned to the header of the complication template. Two simple text providers are then used to assign text to be displayed in the header and body of the complication. Finally, the timeline entry object is created using the template object and an NSDate object set to the current date and time.

28.9 The Complication Data Source Delegate Methods

As previously discussed, the ClockKit framework will make calls to a variety of methods implemented in the complication data source class of the WatchKit app. The purpose of these method calls is to obtain information about the complication timeline and the content of the timeline entries. The data source delegate methods, all of which must be implemented in the delegate class, can be summarized as follows:

28.9.1 getPlaceholderTemplateForComplication:withHandler:

When the user customizes a clock face, the ClockKit framework needs a placeholder template to display in the customization screen. This method will be called by ClockKit once after the app has been installed and is first launched on an Apple Watch. It should return via the provided handler a CLKComplicationTemplate object for the requested complication family populated with suitable placeholder content. The following code shows an example implementation of this method:

```
func getPlaceholderTemplateForComplication(complication: CLKComplication,
withHandler handler: (CLKComplicationTemplate?) -> Void) {

    let template = CLKComplicationTemplateModularLargeStandardBody()

    let beerGlass = UIImage(named: "beer_glass")

    template.headerImageProvider =
        CLKImageProvider(onePieceImage: beerGlass!)
    template.headerTextProvider =
        CLKSimpleTextProvider(text: "Beer Festival")
    template.body1TextProvider =
        CLKSimpleTextProvider(text: "Beer Tasting Schedule")
    handler(template)
}
```

28.9.2 getSupportedTimeTravelDirectionsForComplication:withHandler:

The ClockKit framework calls this method to identify which directions of time travel the complication supports. Acceptable values are as follows:

- **CLKComplicationTimeTravelDirections.None**
- **CLKComplicationTimeTravelDirections.Forward**
- **CLKComplicationTimeTravelDirections.Backward**

If time travel is not supported (in other words the complication only displays one timeline entry configured for the current time) the None option should be specified.

The direction values must be returned via the supplied reply handler method in the form of an options array. The following sample implementation, for example, indicates that both forward and backward time travel are supported:

```
func getSupportedTimeTravelDirectionsForComplication(complication:
CLKComplication, withHandler handler: (CLKComplicationTimeTravelDirections)
-> Void) {
        handler([.Forward, .Backward])
}
```

28.9.3 getTimelineStartDateForComplication:withHandler:

This method is called to request the earliest date for which timeline data is available from the complication. The response is returned via the supplied reply handler in the form of an appropriately configured NSDate object.

28.9.4 getTimelineEndDateForComplication:withHandler:

The ClockKit framework calls this method to obtain the last date for which complication timeline data is available. The response is returned via the supplied reply handler in the form of an appropriately configured NSDate object.

28.9.5 getCurrentTimelineEntryForComplication:withHandler:

When called by the ClockKit framework, this method must return the complication timeline entry object that is to be displayed now.

28.9.6 getTimelineEntriesForComplication:beforeDate:limit:withHandler:

The ClockKit framework uses this method to obtain an array of timeline entries preceding a specified date and time. The method is passed the maximum number of entries to be returned by the method via the reply handler.

28.9.7 getTimelineEntriesForComplication:afterDate:limit:withHandler:

Called by ClockKit to obtain an array of timeline entries occurring after a specified date and time. The method is passed the maximum number of entries to be returned by the method via the reply handler.

28.9.8 getNextRequestedUpdateDateWithHandler:handler:

This method is used to notify the ClockKit framework of the date and time at which an updated timeline should be requested from the complication. The date returned by this method should be as far into the future as possible without impacting the usefulness of the complication.

28.9.9 getPrivacyBehaviorForComplication:withHandler:

This method will be called to obtain the privacy behavior for the complication. This basically amounts to indicating whether the complication data should be visible on the clock face when the device is locked. Supported values that may be returned by this method are as follows:

- **CLKComplicationPrivacyBehavior.ShowOnLockScreen**
- **CLKComplicationPrivacyBehavior.HideOnLockScreen**

28.10 Managing Complications with the CLKComplicationServer Object

The CLKComplicationServer is an object which can be used to gather information about active complications and to request changes to the timeline of a specified complication. CLKComplicationServer is a shared object, a reference to which is obtained as follows:

```
let server = CLKComplicationServer.sharedInstance()
```

Once a reference to the server object has been obtained, an array of active CLKComplication objects for the current app may be obtained via a call to the *activeComplications* method as follows:

```
let activeComplications = server.activeComplications()
```

The CLKComplicationServer object may also be used to request that the timeline for a specified complication be reloaded:

```
server.reloadTimeLineForComplication(complication)
```

When using this method call, it is important to be aware that each WatchKit app is allocated a budget restricting the amount of data a complication can transfer over a given period of time to avoid excessive battery drain. Requests to reload the timeline data should, therefore, be used sparingly.

The timeline for a specified complication may be extended via a call to the *extendTimelineForComplication* method of the server object:

```
server.extendTimelineForComplication(complication)
```

When this method is called, the ClockKit framework will call both the beforeDate and afterDate versions of the *getTimelineEntriesForComplication* methods of the complication data source to obtain the additional timeline entries.

28.11 **Summary**

Complications are small fragments of timeline-based information provided by a WatchKit app which are displayed alongside the time and date in the clock faces of an Apple Watch. Complications are developed using the ClockKit framework and can take the form of a variety of different shapes and sizes. A complication object typically consists of images and text constructed using image and text providers. Once created, the complication object is combined with a date object to create a timeline entry object. Once a timeline has been constructed, the user is able to use the time travel feature to view current, past and future timeline events within the clock faces into which the complication has been embedded.

29. A watchOS 2 ClockKit Complication Tutorial

The previous chapter explored the theory behind the implementation of complications in watchOS 2. This chapter will work through the creation of an example project designed to show the basics steps involved in implementing a complication for a WatchKit app.

29.1 About the Complication Project

The complication created in this project is intended to accompany a WatchKit app developed for a beer festival. At hourly intervals during this festival, different breweries will be hosting special beer tasting sessions. The purpose of the complication is to notify the user of the time of the next tasting, the type of beer being served and the booth number at which that particular brewery is located.

The timeline will contain four events scheduled at hourly intervals starting from the initial invocation of the complication with the information presented using the Modular Large complication family.

29.2 Creating the Complication Project

Start Xcode and create a new iOS project. On the template screen choose the *Application* option located under *watchOS* in the left hand panel and select *iOS App with WatchKit App*. Click *Next,* set the product name to *ClockKitApp,* enter your organization identifier and make sure that the *Devices* menu is set to *Universal.*

Before clicking *Next*, change the *Language* menu to Swift, switch the *Include Complication* option *on* and all other include options *off*.

On the final screen, choose a location in which to store the project files and click on *Create* to proceed to the main Xcode project window.

Choose options for your new project:

Figure 29-1

Within the Project Navigator panel (Figure 29-2), note that Xcode has added an additional Swift class file named *ComplicationController.swift* within the WatchKit extension folder to act as the complication data source class:

Figure 29-2

Select this file and review the template delegate methods that have been generated by Xcode ready to be completed.

29.3 Configuring the Supported Complication Families

The next step in the configuration process is to select the complication families which are to be supported by the WatchKit app extension. To configure these settings, select the *ClockKitApp* target at the top of the Project Navigator panel and select the *General* tab in the main panel. Using the menu in the upper left hand corner of the settings panel, select the *ClockKit WatchKit Extension* entry as shown in Figure 29-3:

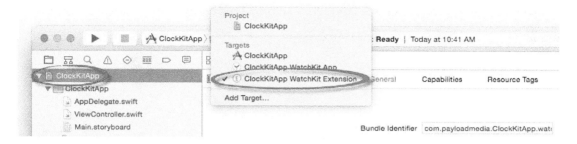

Figure 29-3

Within the general settings for the extension target, locate the *Complications Configuration* section and uncheck all of the supported family options with the exception of the *Modular Large* entry. Also verify that the *Data Source Class* field is set to the correct class (it should read $(PRODUCT_MODULE_NAME).ComplicationController):

▼ **Complications Configuration**

Data Source Class $(PRODUCT_MODULE_NAME).Cc

Supported Families ☐ Modular Small

☑ Modular Large

☐ Utilitarian Small

☐ Utilitarian Large

☐ Circular Small

Complications Group Complication

Figure 29-4

The settings configured in this panel are stored in the *Info.plist* file of the extension target and can be reviewed by selecting this file within the Project Navigator panel. Once selected, the relevant properties will appear in the property editor as shown in Figure 29-5:

CLKComplicationPrincipalClass	⬍	String	$(PRODUCT_MODULE_NAME).ComplicationController
▼ CLKComplicationSupportedFamilies	⬍	Array	(1 item)
Item 0		String	CLKComplicationFamilyModularLarge

Figure 29-5

29.4 **Adding the Data and Image to the Data Source**

The data source for the complication has been designated by Xcode to be the ComplicationController class contained within the *ComplicationController.swift* file. The next step in the project is to add some data to be displayed within the complication timeline. This will take the form of an array object initialized with the text to be displayed within each timeline entry. Locate, select and edit the *ComplicationController.swift* file and modify it to declare this array as follows:

```
import ClockKit

class ComplicationController: NSObject, CLKComplicationDataSource {

    let timeLineText = ["Oatmeal Stout at Booth 212", "Porter at Booth 432",
"Pale Ale at Booth 232", "English Bitter at Booth 327"]
    .
    .
    .
}
```

The complication is also going to display an image of a pint glass in the header of the message. This icon image file is named *beer_glass.png* and can be found in the *image_files* folder of the sample code download available from the following link:

http://www.ebookfrenzy.com/print/watchos2/index.php

Locate this image file in a Finder window and drag and drop it onto the Project Navigator panel beneath the *ClockKit WatchKit Extension* entry as shown in Figure 29-6:

Figure 29-6

29.5 Implementing the Placeholder Delegate Method

When the WatchKit app is first installed on an Apple Watch, the *getPlaceholderTemplateForComplication* method in the *ComplicationController.swift* file will be called and required to return the placeholder template for the complication. This is the complication that will be displayed when the user customizes the clock face to include the complication. Locate the template method within the *ComplicationController.swift* file and implement the code to create and return the placeholder template:

```
func getPlaceholderTemplateForComplication(complication: CLKComplication,
withHandler handler: (CLKComplicationTemplate?) -> Void) {

    let template = CLKComplicationTemplateModularLargeStandardBody()
    let beerGlass = UIImage(named: "beer_glass")

    template.headerImageProvider =
            CLKImageProvider(onePieceImage: beerGlass!)

    template.headerTextProvider =
        CLKSimpleTextProvider(text: "Beer Festival")
    template.body1TextProvider =
        CLKSimpleTextProvider(text: "Beer Tasting Schedule")

    handler(template)
}
```

The code added to this method creates a new complication template object based on the standard large modular family and then uses image and text providers to set the image and text content of the placeholder. The reply handler is then called and used to return the template object to the ClockKit framework.

29.6 Configuring Travel Directions

The ClockKit framework time travel feature needs to know the directions in which it will be able to traverse the timeline. For the purposes of the example, the timeline will only contain future events. As such the *getSupportedTimeTravelDirectionsForComplication* method needs to be modified to support only forward direction time travel:

```
func getSupportedTimeTravelDirectionsForComplication(complication:
CLKComplication, withHandler handler: (CLKComplicationTimeTravelDirections)
-> Void) {

    handler([.Forward])
}
```

With this property configured for forward travel only, the complication in the clock face will be dimmed out in the event the user attempts to travel into the past.

29.7 Adding a Timeline Entry Creation Method

A number of the methods in the data source class will need to create complication timeline entries. Rather than duplicate code in multiple methods it is more efficient to write a single utility method and call that whenever a timeline entry is needed. This method will be named *createTimeLineEntry* and will take as parameters the header and body text to be included in the complication and the date of the timeline entry in the form of an NSDate object. The code for the method will also incorporate the beer glass icon into the entry before returning the result in the form of a completed CLKComplicationTimelineEntry object. Within the *ComplicationController.swift* file, implement this method as follows:

```
func createTimeLineEntry(headerText: String, bodyText: String, date: NSDate)
-> CLKComplicationTimelineEntry {

    let template = CLKComplicationTemplateModularLargeStandardBody()
    let beerGlass = UIImage(named: "beer_glass")

    template.headerImageProvider =
        CLKImageProvider(onePieceImage: beerGlass!)
    template.headerTextProvider = CLKSimpleTextProvider(text: headerText)
    template.body1TextProvider = CLKSimpleTextProvider(text: bodyText)

    let entry = CLKComplicationTimelineEntry(date: date,
            complicationTemplate: template)

    return(entry)
}
```

The method takes the same steps as those outlined for the *getPlaceholderTemplateForComplication* method to create a complication template object and combines that object with the designated date to create a timeline entry object.

29.8 Specifying the Timeline Start and End Dates

Among the information required by the ClockKit framework for a complication are the start and end dates of the timeline. In this example, the start date is the first timeline entry which will be displayed for the current time. The *getTimelineStartDateForComplication* method, therefore, simply needs to return the current date and time:

```
func getTimelineStartDateForComplication(complication: CLKComplication,
withHandler handler: (NSDate?) -> Void) {

    let currentDate = NSDate()
    handler(currentDate)
}
```

Since the timeline contains four entries spaced at hourly intervals, the *getTimelineEndDateForComplication* method needs to calculate and return a time four hours into the future from the current time:

```
func getTimelineEndDateForComplication(complication: CLKComplication,
withHandler handler: (NSDate?) -> Void) {

    let currentDate = NSDate()
    let endDate =
        currentDate.dateByAddingTimeInterval(NSTimeInterval(4 * 60 * 60))

    handler(endDate)
}
```

29.9 Providing the Current Timeline Entry

Once the user has added the complication into a clock face the ClockKit framework will request the timeline entry to be displayed for the current time. It does this via a call to the *getCurrentTimelineEntryForComplication* method of the complication data source. The code for this method now needs to be added to the template method in the *ComplicationController.swift* file as follows:

```
func getCurrentTimelineEntryForComplication(complication: CLKComplication,
withHandler handler: ((CLKComplicationTimelineEntry?) -> Void)) {

    if complication.family == .ModularLarge {
        let dateFormatter = NSDateFormatter()
        dateFormatter.dateFormat = "hh:mm"

        let timeString = dateFormatter.stringFromDate(NSDate())

        let entry = createTimeLineEntry(timeString, bodyText:
timeLineText[0], date: NSDate())

        handler(entry)
    } else {
        handler(nil)
    }
}
```

The method begins by checking that the requested complication family matches the modular large family. A date formatter object is then created and used to create a string containing the current time in hh:mm format. This string, together with the first entry from the timeLineText array and an NSDate object set to the current time is then passed to the *createTimeLineEntry* utility method. The returned timeline entry object is then passed back to the ClockKit framework via the reply handler. In the event that a complication family other than modular large is selected, a nil value is returned to indicate that no entry is available.

29.10 **Providing the Remaining Timeline Entries**

Because the complication in this tutorial only supports forward time travel, it is only necessary to implement the *getTimelineEntriesForComplication:afterDate* method in the *ComplicationController.swift* file, leaving the *beforeDate* variant of the method returning a nil value:

```
func getTimelineEntriesForComplication(complication: CLKComplication,
afterDate date: NSDate, limit: Int, withHandler handler:
(([CLKComplicationTimelineEntry]?) -> Void)) {

    var timeLineEntryArray = [CLKComplicationTimelineEntry]()
    var nextDate = NSDate(timeIntervalSinceNow: 1 * 60 * 60)

    for index in 1...3 {

        let dateFormatter = NSDateFormatter()
        dateFormatter.dateFormat = "hh:mm"

        let timeString = dateFormatter.stringFromDate(nextDate)

        let entry = createTimeLineEntry(timeString, bodyText:
timeLineText[index], date: nextDate)

        timeLineEntryArray.append(entry)

        nextDate = nextDate.dateByAddingTimeInterval(1 * 60 * 60)
    }
    handler(timeLineEntryArray)
}
```

The code begins by creating and initializing an array of CLKComplicationTimelineEntry objects and calculating the date of the next entry (in this case an hour into the future from the current time). A *for* loop is then used to iterate through the remaining three entries in the timeLineText array, formatting the time for each entry and calling the *createTimeLineEntry* method with the text and date values. Once a timeline entry has been created it is added to the timeLineEntryArray array and the date incremented by an additional hour. Once all of the entries have been placed into the array it is returned to the ClockKit framework via the reply handler.

The code for the complication is now complete and ready for testing.

29.11 Adding the Complication to a Clock Face

Before the complication will be visible to the user it must be added to a clock face on the Apple Watch device. From the Xcode toolbar, select the *Complication – ClockKitApp WatchKit App* target and run it either on a physical Apple Watch device or Watch Simulator session.

On the watch or simulator display the time and perform a deep press on the screen (to make a deep press on the simulator, select the *Hardware -> Force Touch Pressure -> Deep Press* menu option, click on the screen then switch back to *Shallow Press* mode).

When the clock face customization screen appears make swiping motions until the *Modular* clock face shown in Figure 29-7 appears:

Figure 29-7

Tap on the *Customize* button to display the color configuration screen and then swipe left to display the complications configuration screen (Figure 29-8):

Figure 29-8

Select the center modular large complication and use the Digital Crown (or mouse scroll wheel if using the simulator) to scroll through the available complications until the *ClockKitApp WatchKit App* complication appears showing the placeholder content:

Figure 29-9

Press the Digital Crown to save the selection then tap on the clock face selection screen to return to the live clock face.

29.12 Testing the Complication

With the complication included in the clock face, the current timeline entry should be visible as illustrated in Figure 29-10:

Figure 29-10

Test the time travel feature using either the Digital Crown on the Apple Watch, or by clicking the time display in the simulator and using the mouse scroll wheel. Traveling back in time should cause the complication to dim. Forward time travel, on the other hand, should move through the future timeline entries:

Figure 29-11

Travelling beyond the last timeline entry will once again cause the complication to be dimmed to indicate that there are no further events to display.

29.13 Summary

This chapter has worked through the creation of a project that demonstrates the practical steps involved in implementing a ClockKit complication for a WatchKit app. The steps covered included the creation of a project containing a complication, the selection of the supported complication families and the implementation of the delegate methods in the complication data source class including providing a placeholder template and both current and future timeline entries. The complication was then added to a watchOS 2 clock face and tested in terms of displaying the current timeline entry and future entries using the time travel feature.

Chapter 30

30. Supporting Different Apple Watch Display Sizes

The Apple Watch family currently consists of two sizes of device in the form of 38mm and 42mm models. Although the difference in screen sizes between the two models is a mere 4mm, this is sufficient difference that a scene layout that fits perfectly on a 42mm Apple Watch may not fit on the 38mm model. It will frequently be necessary, therefore, to have different user interface layout attributes for each Apple Watch model. In addition to handling different screen sizes, a WatchKit app may also optionally display text using the user's preferred font size setting.

Fortunately both the WatchKit framework and Interface Builder tool make it relatively easy to adapt scene layouts to accommodate different screen sizes and font preference settings.

30.1 Screen Size Customization Attributes

Attributes are set on user interface objects within Interface Builder by selecting the object in the storyboard scene and making changes in the Attributes Inspector panel. By default, attributes set in this way are applied to the scene when running on both sizes of Apple Watch. While designing WatchKit app scenes it is quite common, however, to need to specify a different attribute value for the 38mm screen than for the 42mm screen. Fortunately, the Attributes Inspector panel provides a mechanism for configuring *screen size customization attributes*. These are attributes that will be applied to the selected interface object only when the app is run on a specific screen size.

Attributes that are eligible to have screen size customization values configured appear within the Attributes Inspector panel with a small "+" button positioned in the left margin as highlighted in Figure 30-1:

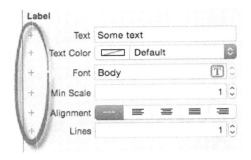

Figure 30-1

When clicked, these buttons display a menu (Figure 30-2) allowing a screen size to be selected:

Figure 30-2

Once a screen size customization attribute has been added to an interface object it appears as an additional option within the Attributes Inspector panel. Figure 30-3, for example, shows a font setting customization attribute that configures a label object to use a smaller font size when the app runs on a 38mm Apple Watch:

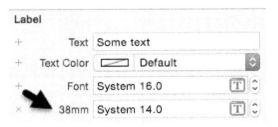

Figure 30-3

The general rule with customization attributes is that the default setting is applied on all screen sizes unless specifically overridden by a customization attribute. In the above figure, for example, the label will display text using the 16pt system font on the 42mm watch model. When running on the smaller 38mm watch model, however, the 14pt customization font attribute will be used. It is worth noting that it is not necessary to also add a customization attribute for the 42mm font setting since this is covered by the default value.

30.2 Working with Screen Sizes in Interface Builder

By default, the storyboard editor in Interface Builder displays storyboard scenes in *Any Screen Size* mode. When in this mode, interface objects are displayed using the default attributes. To see how the scenes within a storyboard will appear on different screen sizes, this mode can be changed using the selection at the bottom of the storyboard editor panel as shown in Figure 30-4:

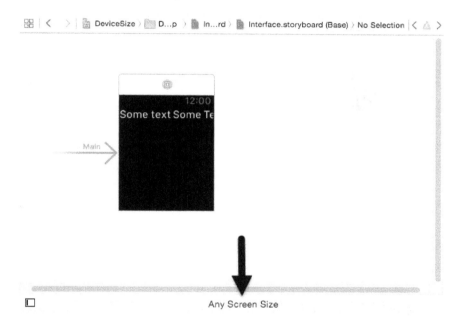

Figure 30-4

Clicking on the button displays a menu of screen size options which, when selected, change the mode of the storyboard canvas to match the chosen screen size.

When a specific screen size mode is selected in Interface Builder the scenes in the canvas will update to reflect the size of the screen. In addition, the interface objects within the scenes will change to reflect any customization attributes that have been set for the selected screen size. This allows you to review the user interface layout as it will appear when running on the designated Apple Watch model.

A more significant point to note about changing the storyboard screen size mode is that any changes made to the scene layout will apply only for the current screen size. Consider, for example, a scene containing a label. If the storyboard editor is in 38mm mode when the text of the label is changed within the scene then that change only applies to the layout when the app is running on a 38mm device. In other words, visually manipulating the objects and layout when the storyboard editor is set for a specific screen size essentially configures screen size customization attributes which also appear within the Attributes Inspector panel.

In Figure 30-5, for example, the text displayed on a label has been changed to read "My 42mm Text" from within the scene canvas while the storyboard editor is in 42mm mode. Note that as a result of this change a matching 42mm screen size customization attribute for the text property is now listed in the Attributes Inspector panel:

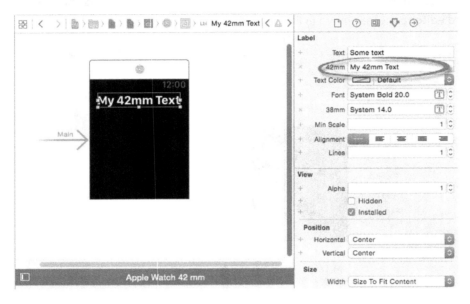

Figure 30-5

Clearly, screen size customization attributes can be configured both manually by adding custom attributes via the Attributes Inspector panel and visually from within the storyboard editor by changing the screen size mode and directly manipulating the interface objects.

When the storyboard editor is in any mode other than *Any Screen Size*, the toolbar at the bottom of the canvas is displayed in blue. This is intended as a subtle reminder that any changes made in this mode will apply only to the currently selected screen size. This includes the addition and deletion of interface objects from the canvas.

As a general rule, screen size customization attributes should be used only when a default setting will not work for both screen sizes. A useful approach is to choose a screen size as the baseline for the layout (for example the 42mm size) and design the user interface using default attributes. The layout can then be adapted for the smaller screen size by overriding the default settings only where necessary for the 38mm screen.

Apple also recommends changing the layout as little as possible between screen sizes to ensure a consistent look to the app on different devices. Drastic alterations that significantly change the appearance of the app user interface from one screen size to another should be avoided.

30.3 Identifying the Screen Size at Runtime

When developing WatchKit apps it is often necessary to make dynamic changes to the interface objects in a scene at runtime. Clearly such changes need to take into consideration the size of the screen on which the app is currently running. This can be achieved using the WKInterfaceDevice class. This class provides interface controllers with access to information about the watch device such as the size of the screen.

The first step in obtaining the current screen size is to get a reference to the current device object as follows:

```
let sharedDevice = WKInterfaceDevice.currentDevice()
```

Once a reference to the shared device object has been obtained the screen bounds property can be accessed:

```
let bounds = device.screenBounds
```

The bounds property is stored as a CGRect value from which the height and width dimensions of the screen can be accessed:

```
let height = bounds.height
let width = bounds.width
```

The screen dimension of the two Apple Watch models are as follows:

- Apple Watch 38mm – Height: 170 / Width: 136
- Apple Watch 42mm – Height: 195 / Width: 156

30.4 Summary

Although limited to two display sizes, steps will often still need to be taken to customize aspects of a scene layout to accommodate both the 38mm and 42mm Apple Watch models. This chapter has outlined the features of Interface Builder that are designed specifically for the purpose of creating scene layouts that adapt to the display size of the device on which the app is running.

31. A WatchKit Map Tutorial

WatchKit currently provides limited support for displaying maps within an app running on an Apple Watch device. The features offered by the WKInterfaceMap class consist of the ability to display a designated map region and to add annotations in the form of colored pins or custom images at specified locations within the defined region. When tapped by the user, the Map object opens the built-in Apple Watch Map app configured to display the same region. The situation has improved slightly with watchOS 2 in that the Core Location framework is now available for use within the WatchKit extension. As will be demonstrated in this chapter, this allows tasks such as obtaining the user's current location to be performed from within the WatchKit extension without the need to request the information from the companion iOS app.

The remainder of this chapter will work through a basic tutorial designed to highlight some of the key features of the WKInterfaceMap class. The project will demonstrate the use of the Core Location framework to obtain current location information and use it to display the current location as an annotation within a WKInterfaceMap object.

31.1 Creating the Example Map Project

Start Xcode and create a new iOS project. On the template screen choose the *Application* option located under *watchOS* in the left hand panel and select *iOS App with WatchKit App*. Click *Next,* set the product name to *MapDemoApp,* enter your organization identifier and make sure that the *Devices* menu is set to *Universal*. Before clicking *Next*, change the *Language* menu to Swift and switch off all of the *Include* options. On the final screen, choose a location in which to store the project files and click on *Create* to proceed to the main Xcode project window.

31.2 Designing the WatchKit App User Interface

Select the *Interface.storyboard* file and drag and drop a Map and Slider object from the Object Library onto the scene canvas so that the layout matches that shown in Figure 31-1:

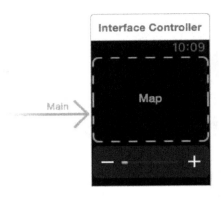

Figure 31-1

Select the Slider object, display the Attributes Inspector and configure the following property values:

- **Value:** 1
- **Minimum:** 1
- **Maximum:** 10
- **Steps:** 10

Display the Assistant Editor and establish an outlet connection from the Map object named *mapObject*. With the Assistant Editor still displayed, establish an action connection from the Slider object to a method named *changeMapRegion*.

31.3 **Configuring the Containing iOS App**

Before any application can begin to track location information when running in the background it must first seek permission to do so from the user. This can be achieved by making a call to the *requestWhenInUseAuthorization* method of the CLLocationManager instance.

Select the *InterfaceController.swift* file for the WatchKit extension target and modify the code to import the CoreLocation framework, store a reference to the CLLocationManager instance and call the *requestWhenInUseAuthorization* method within the *awakeWithContext* method:

```
import WatchKit
import Foundation
import CoreLocation

class InterfaceController: WKInterfaceController {

    @IBOutlet var mapObject: WKInterfaceMap!
    var locationManager: CLLocationManager = CLLocationManager()
```

```
override func awakeWithContext(context: AnyObject?) {
    super.awakeWithContext(context)

    locationManager.requestWhenInUseAuthorization()
}
.
.
.
}
```

The *requestWhenInUseAuthorization* method call requires that a specific key-value pair be added to the Information Property List dictionary contained within the application's Info.plist file. The value takes the form of a string describing the reason why the application needs access to the user's current location. In the case of background access to location information, the *NSLocationWhenInUseUsageDescription* key must be added to the property list.

Within the Project Navigator panel, load the *Info.plist* file (the one located under the *MapDemoApp* target, not either of the WatchKit target *Info.plist* files) into the editor. The key-value pair needs to be added to the *Information Property List* dictionary. Select this entry in the list and click on the + button to add a new entry to the dictionary. Within the new entry, enter *NSLocationWhenInUseUsageDescription* into the key column and, once the key has been added, double-click in the corresponding value column and enter the following text:

```
This information is required to identify your current location
```

Once the entry has been added to the Info.plist file it should appear as illustrated in Figure 31-2:

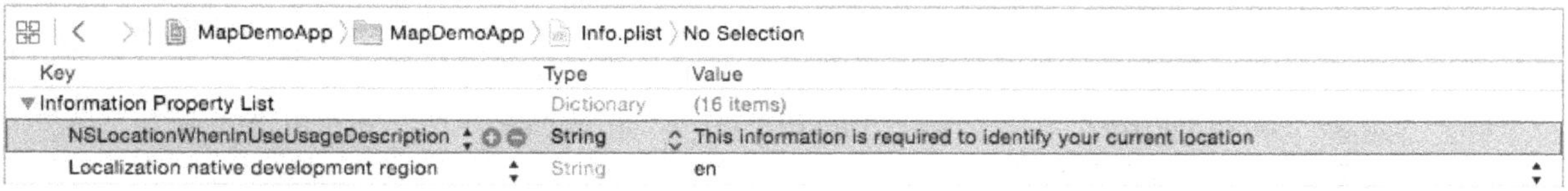

Key	Type	Value
▼ Information Property List	Dictionary	(16 items)
NSLocationWhenInUseUsageDescription	String	This information is required to identify your current location
Localization native development region	String	en

Figure 31-2

The WatchKit app must now be run and the location tracking request approved. Select *MapDemoApp WatchKit App* in the Xcode run target menu and launch the app on a device or simulator session. The first time that the app is launched, the system will display a message on the Apple Watch indicating that permission must be given on the iPhone device to track location information (Figure 31-3). Using the paired iPhone tap the *Allow* button on the request panel to enable this access.

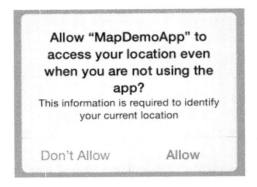

Figure 31-3

31.4 Getting the Current Location

The next step is to instruct the location manager to request the user's current location. This involves declaring the InterfaceController class as implementing the CLLocationManagerDelegate protocol, assigning the class as the delegate for the location manager and then the location update. Note that the code also declares a variable in which to store the current map location:

```
import WatchKit
import Foundation
import CoreLocation

class InterfaceController: WKInterfaceController, CLLocationManagerDelegate
{

    @IBOutlet var mapObject: WKInterfaceMap!
    var locationManager: CLLocationManager = CLLocationManager()
    var mapLocation: CLLocationCoordinate2D?

    override func awakeWithContext(context: AnyObject?) {
        super.awakeWithContext(context)

        locationManager.requestWhenInUseAuthorization()
        locationManager.desiredAccuracy = kCLLocationAccuracyBest
        locationManager.delegate = self
        locationManager.requestLocation()
    }
    .
    .
    .
}
```

When the location manager receives a location update, it will call the *didUpdateLocations* method on the delegate. This class now needs to be implemented in the *InterfaceController.swift* file along with the *didFailWithError* delegate method as follows:

```
func locationManager(manager: CLLocationManager, didUpdateLocations
locations: [CLLocation]) {

    let currentLocation = locations[0]
    let lat = currentLocation.coordinate.latitude
    let long = currentLocation.coordinate.longitude

    self.mapLocation = CLLocationCoordinate2DMake(lat, long)

    let span = MKCoordinateSpanMake(0.1, 0.1)

    let region = MKCoordinateRegionMake(self.mapLocation!, span)
    self.mapObject.setRegion(region)

    self.mapObject.addAnnotation(self.mapLocation!,
                    withPinColor: .Red)
}

func locationManager(manager: CLLocationManager, didFailWithError error:
NSError) {

    print(error.description)
}
```

The code begins by accessing the current location data from the array passed to the method and extracting the latitude and longitude values.

These values are then used to create a CLLocationCoordinate2D object which is stored in the previously declared *mapLocation* variable:

```
self.mapLocation = CLLocationCoordinate2DMake(lat, long)
```

Next a span value is defined to dictate the area that will be covered by the map region. This is then used along with the current location to create the region that will be displayed by the map:

```
let span = MKCoordinateSpanMake(0.1, 0.1)
let region = MKCoordinateRegionMake(self.mapLocation!, span)
```

Finally, the map object is configured to display the region and a red pin added to mark the current location:

```
self.mapObject.setRegion(region)
self.mapObject.addAnnotation(self.mapLocation!, withPinColor: .Red)
```

The color of the pin is specified using the *WKInterfaceMapPinColor* constant which provides the following color options:

- WKInterfaceMapPinColor.Red
- WKInterfaceMapPinColor.Green
- WKInterfaceMapPinColor.Purple

With these changes made to the interface controller class, compile and run the WatchKit app which, when running, should display a map region centered around the user's current location as shown in Figure 31-4:

Figure 31-4

When running in the simulator, the location will be based on the current setting of the *Debug -> Location* menu.

31.5 Adding Zooming Support

A zooming effect can be added to a map by enlarging and reducing the currently displayed region. For the purposes of this example, the current region will be modified by the Slider object. Previously in this chapter the Slider object in the WatchKit app scene was connected to an action method named *changeMapRegion*. Edit the *InterfaceController.swift* file, locate this method and modify it as follows to change the region span based on the current slider setting:

```
@IBAction func changeMapRegion(value: Float) {

    let degrees:CLLocationDegrees = CLLocationDegrees(value / 10)
```

```
        let span = MKCoordinateSpanMake(degrees, degrees)
        let region = MKCoordinateRegionMake(mapLocation!, span)

        mapObject.setRegion(region)
}
```

Run the WatchKit app again and check that changes to the Slider object are reflected in the currently displayed map region giving the effect of zooming in and out of the map.

31.6 Summary

Maps are represented in WatchKit by the WKInterfaceMap class. This class is limited to displaying a static map region together with optional annotation markers in the form of pins or custom images. Tapping on the map launches the built-in Apple Watch Map app configured to display the same region where a wider range of options are available to the user.

This chapter has worked through the creation of an example project intended to highlight the basic features of the WKInterfaceMap class and to demonstrate the use of the Core Location framework in obtaining location data on behalf of the Map object.

32. An Overview of Notifications in WatchKit

W hen an iOS app receives a notification, the operating system will decide whether the user should be notified of this event on the iPhone or the paired Apple Watch device. If, for example, the iPhone is currently locked and the user is wearing and has recently interacted with the Apple Watch, the notification will most likely be delivered to the watch.

Not all iOS apps receive notifications, of course, but for those that do it is important that the companion WatchKit app handle those notifications appropriately.

32.1 Default WatchKit Notification Handling

For many WatchKit apps it may not be necessary to make any changes to support notifications. In fact, the only step necessary to provide basic notification support for a WatchKit app is to add appropriately sized notification icons within the AppIcon image set of the WatchKit app bundle.

By default, if a notification arrives for an iOS app with a companion WatchKit app, the system will first decide whether to display the alert on the iPhone or the Apple Watch. In the event that the notification is delivered to the Apple Watch a "short-look" notification scene will first be displayed. This consists of the app icon, the title from the notification and the name of the WatchKit app.

A few seconds after the short-look notification has displayed, the long-look notification panel will appear. By default, this contains a smaller app icon, the name of the app, and the title and alert text from the notification. In addition, a Dismiss button is included which, when tapped, closes the notification and returns the user to the previous activity. Tapping anywhere else on the notification scene launches the WatchKit app associated with the notification. Figure 32-1, for example, shows a typical default long-look notification:

Figure 32-1

All of the default functionality outlined so far is provided without making any code changes to the WatchKit app. It is, however, possible to add additional capabilities to notification handling for the WatchKit app. Perhaps the most common requirement is the addition of *notification action* buttons.

32.2 Creating Notification Actions

Notifications within an iOS app can be configured to add action buttons which appear within the notification panel and, when tapped by the user, trigger application specific actions. If the iOS app has a companion WatchKit app, these same notification action buttons also appear within the long-look notification on the Apple Watch device. Figure 32-2, for example, shows a long-look notification which has been scrolled up to reveal two action buttons in addition to the default "Dismiss" button:

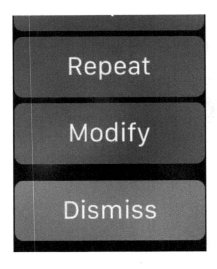

Figure 32-2

Notification actions are configured from within the code of the containing iOS app using a multi-step process. The code to configure the notification actions will need to be executed each time the iOS app runs, so is typically executed in the *didFinishLaunchingWithOptions* method of the application delegate class.

The first step in adding notification actions is to create a *notification action object* for each action to be added. Each notification action object is created as an instance of the UIMutableUserNotificationAction class which needs to be customized via a range of available properties:

- **identifier** – A string which uniquely identifies the action. This identifier will be referenced in the action handler code to ascertain which action was selected by the user.
- **title** – A string value containing the text that is to appear on the action button within the notification panel.
- **destructive** – A Boolean value indicating whether selection of the action will result in the loss of user data or input. When set to true, this causes the title string on the button to appear in red.
- **authentication** – A Boolean value indicating whether or not the user needs to unlock the device before the action can be performed.
- **activationMode** – Used to indicate whether the action should be performed in the foreground or background. In background mode the containing iOS app is launched in the background to perform the task. When a notification appears on the iPhone device, a foreground mode action causes the iOS app to be launched in the foreground. Selection of a foreground mode action when the notification is delivered to the Apple Watch causes the WatchKit app to be launched.
- **behavior** – Indicates whether or not the action is required to obtain text input from the user.

The following code demonstrates the creation of two notification actions, one configured for background mode and the other for foreground mode:

```
var repeatAction = UIMutableUserNotificationAction()
repeatAction.identifier = "REPEAT_IDENTIFIER"
repeatAction.title = "Repeat"
repeatAction.destructive = false
repeatAction.authenticationRequired = false
repeatAction.activationMode =
          UIUserNotificationActivationMode.Background

var modifyAction = UIMutableUserNotificationAction()
modifyAction.identifier = "MODIFY_IDENTIFIER"
modifyAction.title = "Modify"
modifyAction.destructive = false
modifyAction.authenticationRequired = false
modifyAction.activationMode =
        UIUserNotificationActivationMode.Foreground
```

Once the notification action objects have been created, they need to be packaged into a *notification category object* in the form of an instance of the UIMutableUserNotificationCategory class. As with the notification actions, the category object must have assigned to it a unique identifier string. The following code creates a new notification category containing the above notification action objects:

```
var notificationCategory = UIMutableUserNotificationCategory()

notificationCategory.identifier = "REMINDER_CATEGORY"
notificationCategory.setActions([repeatAction, modifyAction],
            forContext: UIUserNotificationActionContext.Default)
```

Finally, the notification category needs to be bundled into a UIUserNotificationSettings object along with any other required settings and registered with the notification system using the *registerUserNotificationSettings* method of the iOS application's UIApplication instance:

```
let settings = UIUserNotificationSettings(forTypes:
        [UIUserNotificationType.Sound,
         UIUserNotificationType.Alert,
         UIUserNotificationType.Badge],
        categories: [notificationCategory])

application.registerUserNotificationSettings(settings)
```

32.3 Inline Text Replies

A new feature introduced in watchOS 2 and iOS 9 allows the user to input text into a notification and have it delivered to the corresponding app. An action is designated as accepting text input using the *behavior* property of the UIMutableUserNotificationAction instance as follows:

```
let replyAction: UIMutableUserNotificationAction =
        UIMutableUserNotificationAction()
replyAction.identifier = "REPLY_IDENTIFIER"
replyAction.title = "Reply"
replyAction.destructive = false
replyAction.authenticationRequired = false
replyAction.behavior = UIUserNotificationActionBehavior.TextInput
```

When text input is provided by the user within the notification it is passed to the corresponding WatchKit app via one of the action handler methods.

When the user selects a text input action within the notification the standard WatchKit text input controller will appear providing the option to make the input using voice dictation, a selection from a range of preset options or emoji selection. Preset text options can be provided by implementing the *suggestionsForResponseToActionWithIdentifier* method within the notification interface controller class as follows:

```
override func suggestionsForResponseToActionWithIdentifier(identifier:
String, forLocalNotification localNotification: UILocalNotification) ->
[NSAttributedString] {

    let suggestion1 = NSMutableAttributedString(string: "I'm too busy")
    let suggestion2 = NSMutableAttributedString(string: "I'm on my way")
    let suggestions = [suggestion1, suggestion2]

    return suggestions
}
```

32.4 Handling Standard Notification Actions

Notifications are categorized as being either local or remote. A local notification is typically initiated from within the containing iOS app. A remote notification, on the other hand, is sent over the internet to the iPhone from a remote server.

As previously outlined, a notification can appear either on the iPhone device or the paired Apple Watch. When a notification action on an Apple Watch is selected by the user, the handler method that gets called will depend on whether the notification was remote or local in origin and whether the notification action was configured for background or foreground mode.

When a remote notification appears on the Apple Watch and the user selects a background notification action, the following method is called on the application delegate of the containing iOS app:

application:handleActionWithIdentifier:forRemoteNotification:completionHandler:

If the notification is local, however, the following method will be called on the app delegate of the containing iOS app when a background action is selected:

application:handleActionWithIdentifier:forLocalNotification:completionHandler:

When a remote notification appears on the Apple Watch and the user selects a foreground notification action, the WatchKit app will launch and the following method on the extension delegate will be called:

handleActionWithIdentifier:forRemoteNotification:

The same scenario involving a local notification on the Apple Watch will result in the following method being called on the extension delegate of the WatchKit app:

handleActionWithIdentifier:forLocalNotification:

32.5 **Handling Inline Text Reply Actions**

Local notification inline text reply actions trigger the following method on the extension delegate of the WatchKit app:

handleActionWithIdentifier:forLocalNotification:withResponseInfo:

In the event that the notification containing the inline text reply action was remotely initiated, the following method of the extension delegate will be called:

handleActionWithIdentifier:forRemoteNotification:withResponseInfo:

Both methods are passed a string containing the notification category identifier, the notification object and dictionary object containing the text entered by the user. The key to access to the text within the dictionary is UIUserNotificationActionResponseTypedTextKey. The following code, for example, shows an example implementation of the *handleActionWithIdentifier:forLocalNotification:withResponseInfo:* method in which the user's text input is extracted from the dictionary and printed to the console:

```
func handleActionWithIdentifier(identifier: String, forLocalNotification
localNotification: UILocalNotification, withResponseInfo responseInfo:
[NSObject : AnyObject]) {

    let reply = responseInfo[UIUserNotificationActionResponseTypedTextKey]
    print(reply)
}
```

The topics of WatchKit notification handling, action notifications and inline text input will be covered in further detail in the next chapters (*A WatchKit Notification Tutorial*, *A WatchKit Custom Notification Tutorial* and *A WatchKit Inline Notification Text Reply Tutorial*).

32.6 **Responding to Notifications**

When a notification arrives on the Apple Watch, the WatchKit app will be notified via method call. The specific method that is called depends on whether notification is local or remote in origin and whether or not the WatchKit app is currently active.

When the WatchKit app is active when the notification arrives, either the *didReceiveRemoteNotification* or the *didReceiveLocalNotification* method of the *extension delegate* will be called, depending on whether the notification was initiated remotely or locally. These methods are then able to make changes where necessary within the running app in response to the notification.

If the WatchKit app is inactive when the notification is triggered, either the *didReceiveRemoteNotification:withCompletion:* or the *didReceiveLocalNotification:withCompletion:* method of the *notification interface controller* will be called before the notification interface is displayed to the user. When working with custom notifications, these methods will need to update the custom notification scene before calling the supplied completion handler.

32.7 Custom Notifications

The previously outlined default notification handling within WatchKit is somewhat limited in terms of customization options. While it is possible to add action buttons to the notification when it is displayed to the user, there is no control of the layout and content that is presented within the notification scene. This shortcoming can be overcome, however, through the use of custom notifications.

Custom notifications allow the appearance of a notification category on the Apple Watch to be designed in terms of the interface objects that are presented to the user and the content that is displayed on those objects. In fact, a dynamic custom interface can contain any combination of non-interactive interface objects such as Label, Map and Image objects.

A custom notification is made up of two parts referred to as *static* and *dynamic* notifications.

32.8 Dynamic and Static Notifications

Custom notifications consist of a static and a dynamic notification. The static notification consists of a Label object which displays the content of the notification's alert body text. The static notification scene can be customized by adding additional non-interactive interface objects such as Labels and Images (note that any images displayed on the static notification scene must be bundled with the WatchKit app and not the extension), and the attributes of those objects can be customized at design time. Once those attributes have been set, however, there is no way to change the appearance or content displayed on the objects before the static notification appears (hence the term *static*).

An optional dynamic notification may also be added to the static notification. The dynamic notification scene may also be customized in terms of layout and the addition of non-interactive interface objects. The difference with the dynamic notification scene is that it has associated with it a *notification interface controller* (subclassed from WKUserNotificationInterfaceController).

As with a standard interface controller class, the notification interface controller can contain outlets connected to interface objects in the dynamic notification scene. When a notification arrives on the Apple Watch device, the dynamic notification interface controller is launched and passed via a handler method a notification object containing details of the alert.

The notification controller handler method is then given the opportunity to update the dynamic notification scene via outlet connections based on the details of the alert before it is presented to the user.

The decision at runtime as to whether the static or dynamic notification is used to deliver a notification on the Apple Watch is made by watchOS based on a number of factors including the resources available on the watch device and the amount of time it takes the dynamic notification handler method to prepare the scene for display.

32.9 Adding a Custom Notification to a WatchKit App

A custom notification can be added to a WatchKit app at creation time by enabling the *Include Notification Scene* option in the new target options panel as highlighted in Figure 32-3:

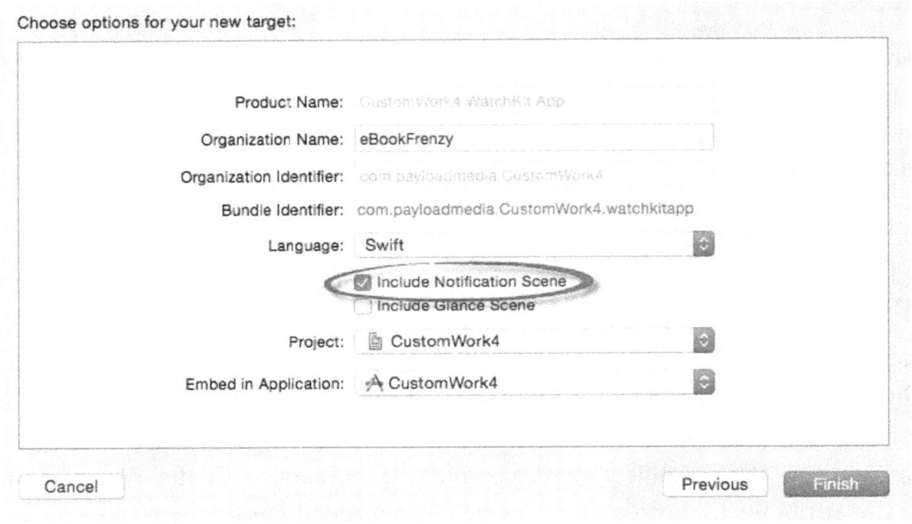

Figure 32-3

Alternatively, a custom notification may be added to an existing project using the following steps:

1. Drag and drop a *Notification Interface Controller* object from the Object Library onto the WatchKit App storyboard canvas.
2. Ctrl-click on the WatchKit Extension folder in the Project Navigator panel, select *New File...* and add a new Cocoa Touch Class to the project subclassed from WKUserNotificationInterfaceController.
3. Select the *Static Interface* scene within the storyboard, display the Attributes Inspector panel and enable the *Has Dynamic Interface* option. This will add the Dynamic Interface scene to the storyboard.
4. Select the newly added Dynamic Interface scene, display the Identity Inspector and change the Class menu to the class added in step 2 above.

Once a custom notification has been added with dynamic support, the scenes will appear in the storyboard as illustrated in Figure 32-4:

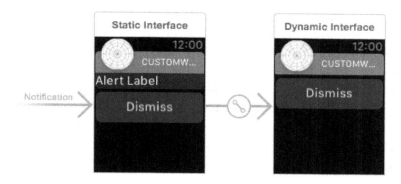

Figure 32-4

32.10 **Configuring the Notification Category**

As previously discussed, notifications have an associated category identifier that is used to differentiate one notification type from another within an app. Custom notifications also have a category identifier which can be specified from within the Document Outline panel. To access and modify the category identifier for a custom notification, select the static notification scene and display the Document Outline panel. Within the Document Outline panel, unfold the *Static Notification Interface Controller* section, select the *Notification Category* entry and, within the Attributes Inspector, change the Name field to the new identifier string:

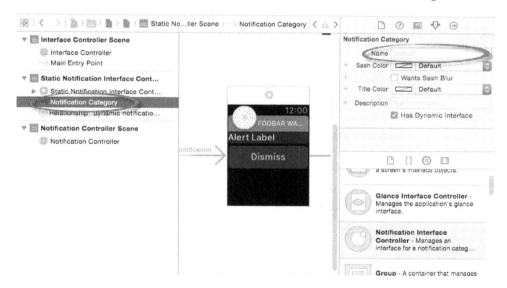

Figure 32-5

Once the custom notification has been assigned a category identifier, that identifier will need to be referenced whenever notification events are configured if those notifications are to be displayed using the custom notification.

32.11 **Updating the Dynamic Notification Scene**

In order for the notification interface controller to be able to dynamically update the interface objects in the dynamic scene, those objects must be connected to outlets. Once those outlets are configured, the code to update the interface needs to be placed in a handler method within the notification interface controller class. By default, Xcode will have placed templates for these methods within the notification interface controller class file. The choice of handler method to use depends on whether the notification is local or remote. For remote notifications the *didReceiveRemoteNotification:withCompletion* method of the notification controller is called by the system while local notifications result in a call to the *didReceiveLocalNotification:withCompletion* handler method.

Each method is passed a notification object from which can be obtained the details of the alert. For local notifications this takes the form of a UILocalNotification object. Remote notifications, on the other hand, receive a Dictionary object containing key-value pairs as defined by the remote notification server.

The handler methods are also passed a reference to a completion handler which must be called once the user interface updates are complete. If the completion handler is not called, or the user interface update takes too long to complete, the system will revert to the static notification.

The topic of custom notifications will be covered in further detail in the chapter entitled *A WatchKit Custom Notification Tutorial*.

32.12 **Summary**

Notifications are a common feature of many iOS applications and are often delivered to the paired Apple Watch, especially if the iPhone device is locked. A considerable amount of notification support is provided by default for WatchKit apps, including the appearance of both short and long-look notification scenes. Notifications can also be extended to include action buttons which can be configured to perform application specific tasks when selected by the user.

Custom notifications may also be used to provide a greater level of control over the layout and content of notifications when delivered to the Apple Watch device.

33. A WatchKit Notification Tutorial

This chapter will create an iOS project containing a WatchKit app that demonstrates the use of the iOS notification system. The example will make use of the standard WatchKit short-look and long-look notification interfaces and include the implementation of a notification action button within the long-look interface.

33.1 About the Example Project

The purpose of the project is to allow the user to trigger a notification alert after a short delay. At the point that the notification appears, the user will be given the opportunity through a notification action button on both the iPhone or Apple Watch device to repeat the notification.

33.2 Creating the Xcode Project

Start Xcode and create a new iOS project. On the template screen choose the *Application* option located under *watchOS* in the left hand panel and select *iOS App with WatchKit App*. Click *Next*, set the product name to *NotifyDemoApp*, enter your organization identifier and make sure that the *Devices* menu is set to *Universal*.

Before clicking *Next*, change the *Language* menu to Swift and switch all of the *Include* options *off* (the Notification Scene option is only required when working with custom notifications, a topic covered in the next chapter).

On the final screen, choose a location in which to store the project files and click on *Create* to proceed to the main Xcode project window.

33.3 Designing the iOS App User Interface

The user interface for the parent iOS app will consist of a single Button object. Select the *Main.storyboard* file and add and configure this object so that the layout matches that illustrated in Figure 33-1, making sure to position the Button in the horizontal center of the layout:

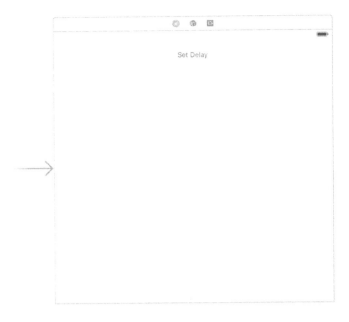

Figure 33-1

Display the *Resolve Auto Layout Issues* menu (Figure 33-2) and select the *Reset to Suggested Constraints* menu option listed under *All Views in View Controller* to establish sensible layout constraints on the button:

Figure 33-2

With the *Main.storyboard* file still loaded into Interface Builder, display the Assistant Editor and establish an action connection from the Button object to a method named *buttonPress*. Review the code in the *ViewController.swift* file and add a constant declaration set to the duration of the delay:

```
import UIKit
```

```
class ViewController: UIViewController {

    let timeValue = 6.0

    override func viewDidLoad() {
        super.viewDidLoad()
    }

    @IBAction func buttonPress(sender: AnyObject) {
    }
    .
    .
    .
}
```

33.4 **Setting the Notification**

A method will now be added to the *ViewController.swift* file to configure the notification using the time delay value with an alert title of "Reminder" and an alert body which reads "Wake Up!". In addition to these settings, the notification will be configured to play the default alert sound and assigned a category identifier of "REMINDER_CATEGORY" (this category will need to be referenced again later in the chapter when action buttons are added to the notification). Remaining in the *ViewController.swift* file, implement this method as outlined in the following listing:

```
func setNotification() {

    let localNotification:UILocalNotification =
                UILocalNotification()

    localNotification.alertTitle = "Reminder"

    localNotification.alertBody = "Wake Up!"

    localNotification.fireDate = NSDate(timeIntervalSinceNow:
                    timeValue)
    localNotification.soundName =
            UILocalNotificationDefaultSoundName
    localNotification.category = "REMINDER_CATEGORY"

    UIApplication.sharedApplication().scheduleLocalNotification(
            localNotification)
}
```

The *setNotification* method will need to be called each time that the user taps the *Set Delay* button which is configured to call the *buttonPressed* method. Add the call to the *setNotification* method within the *buttonPressed* method:

```
@IBAction func buttonPress(sender: AnyObject) {
    setNotification()
}
```

33.5 Adding the Notification Action

When the notification is triggered, the user is to be given the option of repeating the notification using the same delay. This will involve the addition of a notification action to the notification using the "REMINDER_CATEGORY" identifier referenced each time the notification is set. The code to configure the action will be placed within the Application Delegate class within the *didFinishLaunchingWithOptions* method.

Begin by locating and selecting the *AppDelegate.swift* file and modifying the *didFinishLaunchingWithOptions* method to create the notification action as follows:

```
func application(application: UIApplication, didFinishLaunchingWithOptions
launchOptions:
[NSObject: AnyObject]?) -> Bool {

    let repeatAction: UIMutableUserNotificationAction =
            UIMutableUserNotificationAction()
    repeatAction.identifier = "REPEAT_IDENTIFIER"
    repeatAction.title = "Repeat"
    repeatAction.destructive = false
    repeatAction.authenticationRequired = false
    repeatAction.activationMode =
            UIUserNotificationActivationMode.Background

    return true
}
```

The above code creates a new notification action instance and configures it with an identifier string (this will be used to identify which action has been selected by the user later in the project). The action is also configured to display text which reads "Repeat" on the action button and to indicate that it is a non-destructive action (in other words it does not cause the loss of any data or information). In the event that the device is locked when the notification is triggered, the action is configured such that it is not necessary for the user to unlock the device for the action to be performed.

Finally, since the notification can be repeated without the need to display the iOS app, the activation mode is set to *Background* mode.

The next task is to create the notification category containing the action and register it with the notification system:

```
func application(application: UIApplication, didFinishLaunchingWithOptions
launchOptions: [NSObject: AnyObject]?) -> Bool {

    var repeatAction: UIMutableUserNotificationAction =
        UIMutableUserNotificationAction()
    repeatAction.identifier = "REPEAT_IDENTIFIER"
    repeatAction.title = "Repeat"
    repeatAction.destructive = false
    repeatAction.authenticationRequired = false
    repeatAction.activationMode =
        UIUserNotificationActivationMode.Background

    let notificationCategory:UIMutableUserNotificationCategory =
            UIMutableUserNotificationCategory()

    notificationCategory.identifier = "REMINDER_CATEGORY"

    notificationCategory.setActions([repeatAction],
            forContext: UIUserNotificationActionContext.Default)

    let settings = UIUserNotificationSettings(forTypes:
            [UIUserNotificationType.Sound,
             UIUserNotificationType.Alert,
             UIUserNotificationType.Badge],
            categories: [notificationCategory])

    application.registerUserNotificationSettings(settings)

    return true
}
```

Compile and run the iOS app on a physical iPhone device or simulator session, allow notification access if prompted by the operating system and tap the Set Delay button. Once the delay has been set, place the app into the background by pressing the Home button on the device (or selecting the *Hardware -> Home* menu option within the simulator). When the notification appears, swipe downward on the alert panel to display the action button as shown in Figure 33-3:

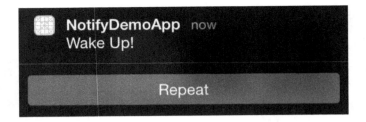

Figure 33-3

Assuming that the notification appears as expected, the next step is to handle the "Repeat" action.

33.6 Implementing the handleActionWithIdentifier Method

When a notification action button configured for background mode is tapped by the user, the *handleActionWithIdentifier* method of the app delegate class is called. Among the items passed to the method are a notification object from which both the action and category identifiers of the action that triggered the call can be obtained together with a completion handler to be called once the action has been handled. This method now needs to be added to the *AppDelegate.swift* file along with a variable in which to store a reference to the view controller instance as follows:

```
@UIApplicationMain
class AppDelegate: UIResponder, UIApplicationDelegate {

    var window: UIWindow?
    var viewController: ViewController?

    func application(application: UIApplication, handleActionWithIdentifier
identifier: String?, forLocalNotification notification: UILocalNotification,
completionHandler: () -> Void) {

        if identifier == "REPEAT_IDENTIFIER" && notification.category ==
"REMINDER_CATEGORY" {
            viewController = ViewController()
            viewController?.setNotification()
        }
        completionHandler()
    }
    .
    .
    .
}
```

The method begins by verifying that the category and action id match the repeat action. If this is a repeat action request, an instance of the ViewController class is created and the *setNotification* method of the instance called to repeat the notification. The completion handler block is then called to indicate that the action has been handled.

Re-run the iOS app, set up a notification and place the app in the background. Display the action button in the notification panel when it appears and tap on the "Repeat" button. After the designated time has elapsed the notification should trigger a second time as requested.

33.7 Adding Notification Icons to the WatchKit App

The WatchKit app requires that six app icons be added to fully support notifications for the Notification Center, Short-Look and Long-Look views. For each icon category, images must be provided for both 38mm and 42mm Apple Watch models. The icons used in the example can be found in the *app_icons* folder of the sample code download available from the following URL:

http://www.ebookfrenzy.com/print/watchos2/index.php

Select the *Assets.xcassets* entry located under *NotifyDemoApp WatchKit App* in the Project Navigator panel and select the *AppIcon* image set as outlined in Figure 33-4:

Figure 33-4

Open a Finder window and navigate to the *app_icons* folder. Once located, drag and drop the following icon image files to the corresponding locations in the image asset catalog:

- **HomeIcon@2x.png** -> Apple Watch Home Screen (All) Long Look (38mm)
- **Notification_Center_38mm@2x.png** -> Apple Watch Notification Center 38mm
- **Notification_Center_42mm@2x.png** -> Apple Watch Notification Center 42mm
- **Long_Look_42mm@2x.png** -> Apple Watch Long Look
- **Short_Look_38mm@2x.png** – Apple Watch Short Look 38mm
- **Short_Look_42mm@2x.png** – Apple Watch Short Look 42mm

33.8 **Testing the Notification on the Apple Watch**

Make sure that the *NotifyDemoApp* target is still selected in the Xcode toolbar and run the iOS app on a physical iPhone device with which an Apple Watch is paired or simulator session. This will launch the iOS app and install the WatchKit app.

Configure a delay, tap the Set Delay button and lock the iPhone device (the simulator can be locked using the *Hardware -> Lock* menu option). Pick up the Apple Watch device so that the screen activates. When the time delay has elapsed, the short look notification should appear on the screen using the designated icon. After a few seconds, the scrollable long look notification should appear including the alert title, alert body, the repeat action button and a Dismiss button:

Figure 33-5

Since the repeat action is already configured to launch the iOS app in the background and re-initiate the notification, tapping the Repeat button on the notification scene of the Apple Watch will cause the notification to repeat.

Make a swiping motion from the top of the watch display to view the Notification Center panel which should also include the notification as illustrated in Figure 33-6:

Figure 33-6

33.9 **Summary**

This chapter has worked through the design and implementation of an example application intended to demonstrate the handling of notifications from within both a containing iOS app and the corresponding WatchKit app with a particular emphasis on the use of notification actions.

34. A WatchKit Custom Notification Tutorial

The previous chapter demonstrated the steps involved in adding action buttons to the default long-look notification scene within a WatchKit app. Although the addition of action notifications provided some additional functionality to the notification, the information displayed to the user was still limited to the alert title and body text. In order to provide a richer experience in terms of presenting information to the user in a notification it is necessary to use a custom notification. This chapter will add to the overview of custom notifications provided in the chapter entitled *An Overview of Notifications in WatchKit* by providing a tutorial based example of the implementation of a custom notification within a WatchKit app.

34.1 About the WatchKit Custom Notification Example

The project created in this chapter will consist of an iOS app with a companion WatchKit app. The iOS app will consist of two buttons which, when selected, will initiate local notifications configured to trigger after a 5 second delay. The WatchKit app that accompanies the iOS app will contain a custom notification which dynamically displays a different image depending on which of the two buttons was used to initiate the notification.

34.2 Creating the Custom Notification Project

Start Xcode and create a new iOS project. On the template screen choose the *Application* option located under *watchOS* in the left hand panel and select *iOS App with WatchKit App.* Click *Next,* set the product name to *CustomNotifyApp,* enter your organization identifier and make sure that the *Devices* menu is set to *Universal.*

On the subsequent screen switch the *Include Notification Scene* on and all other *Include* options off before clicking on the *Finish* button (the Notification Scene option is now required since we are working with custom notifications).

On the final screen, choose a location in which to store the project files and click on *Create* to proceed to the main Xcode project window.

34.3 Designing the iOS App User Interface

The user interface for the parent iOS app will consist of two Button objects. Select the *Main.Storyboard* file and add these objects to the storyboard canvas so that the layout matches that illustrated in Figure 34-1, making sure to position the objects in the horizontal center of the layout:

Figure 34-1

Display the *Resolve Auto Layout Issues* menu (Figure 34-2) and select the *Reset to Suggested Constraints* menu option listed under *All Views in View Controller* to establish sensible layout constraints on the view objects:

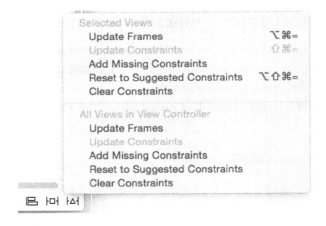

Figure 34-2

With the *Main.storyboard* file still loaded into Interface Builder, display the Assistant Editor and establish action connections from the Rain and Snow button objects to methods named *rainAlert* and *snowAlert* respectively.

34.4 Registering and Setting the Notifications

Select the *AppDelegate.swift* file and modify the *didFinishLaunchingWithOptions* method to register the notification settings for the app. These settings will ensure that the user is prompted by the app the first time it runs to enable access to the notifications system:

```
func application(application: UIApplication, didFinishLaunchingWithOptions
launchOptions: [NSObject: AnyObject]?)
-> Bool {

    let settings = UIUserNotificationSettings(forTypes:
            [UIUserNotificationType.Sound,
             UIUserNotificationType.Alert,
             UIUserNotificationType.Badge], categories: nil)

    application.registerUserNotificationSettings(settings)

    return true
}
```

Next, select the *ViewController.swift* file and add a variable referencing the application context and the code for the two action methods to configure the notifications:

```
import UIKit

class ViewController: UIViewController {

    let app = UIApplication.sharedApplication()

    override func viewDidLoad() {
        super.viewDidLoad()
        // Do any additional setup after loading the view, typically from a
nib.
    }

    @IBAction func rainAlert(sender: AnyObject) {
        let alertTime = NSDate().dateByAddingTimeInterval(5)

        let notifyAlarm = UILocalNotification()

        notifyAlarm.fireDate = alertTime
        notifyAlarm.timeZone = NSTimeZone.defaultTimeZone()
        notifyAlarm.soundName = UILocalNotificationDefaultSoundName
        notifyAlarm.category = "WEATHER_CATEGORY"
        notifyAlarm.alertTitle = "Rain"
        notifyAlarm.alertBody = "It is going to rain"
        app.scheduleLocalNotification(notifyAlarm)
    }
```

```
@IBAction func snowAlert(sender: AnyObject) {
    let alertTime = NSDate().dateByAddingTimeInterval(5)

    let notifyAlarm = UILocalNotification()

    notifyAlarm.fireDate = alertTime
    notifyAlarm.timeZone = NSTimeZone.defaultTimeZone()
    notifyAlarm.soundName = UILocalNotificationDefaultSoundName
    notifyAlarm.category = "WEATHER_CATEGORY"
    notifyAlarm.alertTitle = "Snow"
    notifyAlarm.alertBody = "It is going to snow"
    app.scheduleLocalNotification(notifyAlarm)
}
  .
  .
  .
}
```

Note that both of the notifications have been configured with a category of "WEATHER_CATEGORY". It is essential that this category be referenced in the custom notification on the WatchKit app later in the tutorial.

Compile and run the app on an iPhone device and click on "Allow" when the system requests access to notifications. Once access has been allowed, tap on the Rain button and lock the device. After 5 seconds the alert should appear on the lock screen. Repeat these steps to test that the Snow button notification also works.

34.5 Configuring the Custom Notification

Within the Project Navigator panel, select the *Interface.storyboard* file and locate the notification scenes as illustrated in Figure 34-3:

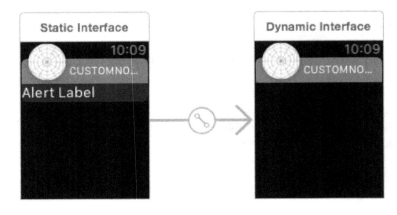

Figure 34-3

The left hand scene is the static scene. By default this is configured with a Label object which will display the content of the alert body text when a notification arrives. For the purposes of this example, no other static content is required on the static notification scene. Before designing the dynamic notification scene, the notification category for the custom notification needs to be changed to match that referenced when the notifications were setup in the iOS View Controller.

Display the Document Outline panel using the button indicated by the arrow in Figure 34-4 and unfold the section entitled *Static Notification Interface Controller*. Within this section of the panel select the *Notification Category* entry (may also read *myCategory*) and, within the Attributes Inspector, change the Name field to *WEATHER_CATEGORY*:

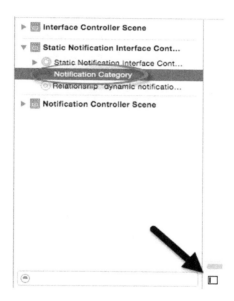

Figure 34-4

34.6 Designing the Dynamic Notification Scene

Remaining within the storyboard, drag a Label object from the Object Library and drop it above the Dismiss button in the Dynamic Interface scene. Select the Label object and, using the Attributes Inspector panel, set the *Alignment* setting in the Label section of the panel to center the text within the label. Within the Alignment section of the panel set the *Horizontal* property to the *Center* setting.

Drag and drop an Image object so that it is positioned beneath the Label object and set the Mode property to *Aspect Fit* and the *Horizontal* Alignment property to *Center*. On completion of these steps the layout of the Dynamic Interface scene should match Figure 34-5:

Figure 34-5

Display the Assistant Editor, verify that it is displaying the *NotificationController.swift* file and establish an outlet connection from the Label object named *notificationAlertLabel*.

Establish a second outlet, this time connected to the Image object and named *notificationImage*. On completion of these steps the top of the *NotificationController.swift* file should read as follows:

```swift
class NotificationController: WKUserNotificationInterfaceController {

    @IBOutlet weak var notificationAlertLabel: WKInterfaceLabel!
    @IBOutlet weak var notificationImage: WKInterfaceImage!

    override init() {
        // Initialize variables here.
        super.init()

        // Configure interface objects here.
    }
    .
    .
    .
}
```

34.7 Configuring the didReceiveLocalNotification method

When a notification alert arrives, the *didReceiveLocalNotification* method of the notification interface controller instance will be called and passed a UILocalNotification object containing details of the alert. A template for this method has already been added by Xcode to the *NotificationController.swift* file but is currently commented out. Open the *NotificationController.swift* file (located in the Project Navigator panel under *CustomNotifyApp WatchKit Extension*), locate this method and remove the /* and */ comment markers positioned before and after the method.

With the method uncommented, implement code as follows to identify whether a rain or snow alert has been triggered and to display a different image on the Image object depending on the alert type:

```
override func didReceiveLocalNotification(localNotification:
UILocalNotification, withCompletion completionHandler:
((WKUserNotificationInterfaceType) -> Void)) {

    if localNotification.alertTitle == "Rain" {
        notificationAlertLabel.setText("Rain")
        notificationImage.setImageNamed("rain_image")
    }

    if localNotification.alertTitle == "Snow" {
        notificationAlertLabel.setText("Snow")
        notificationImage.setImageNamed("snow_image")
    }

    completionHandler(.Custom)
}
```

Note the completion handler call at the end of the method. This notifies the system that the dynamic scene is ready to be displayed. If the completion handler does not get called or the code to configure the scene takes too long to complete, the system will revert to and display the static notification scene.

34.8 Adding the Images to the WatchKit App Bundle

The two images referenced in the *didReceiveLocalNotification* method now need to be added to the project. When configuring a dynamic notification scene, speed is essential to avoid the static notification scene appearing. In order to provide the app with quick access to the image files they will be added to the WatchKit app bundle as named images. The images used in this tutorial reside in the *weather_images* folder of the sample code download available from:

http://www.ebookfrenzy.com/print/watchos2/index.php

Within the Xcode Project Navigator panel locate the *Assets.xcassets* entry listed under *CustomNotifyApp WatchKit App* so that the image catalog loads into the main panel. Ctrl-click in the left hand panel beneath the AppIcon entry and select *Import...* from the resulting menu. In the file selection panel, navigate to and select the *weather_images* folder before clicking on the *Open* button. Once imported, the images should appear in the image set as shown in Figure 34-6:

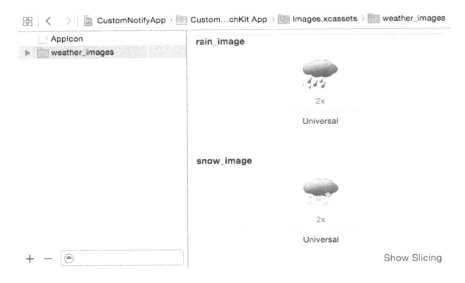

Figure 34-6

34.9 Testing the Custom Notification

If the run target in the Xcode toolbar is currently set to *CustomNotifyApp WatchKit App*, change it back to the *CustomNotifyApp* setting and run the iOS app on an iPhone device with which an Apple Watch is paired. When the iOS app main screen appears tap the Rain button and lock the device. Pick up the paired Apple Watch so that the screen activates and wait for the notification to appear, at which point it should display the rain cloud image as shown in Figure 34-7:

Figure 34-7

Scroll down within the notification scene and tap the Dismiss button to close the notification. Repeat the above steps, this time selecting the Snow button. This time the notification should appear on the Apple Watch using the snow cloud image. The app is now successfully using a dynamic custom notification.

34.10 Summary

Custom notifications provide a considerable amount of control over the content contained within a notification when it appears on an Apple Watch device. This chapter has worked through the creation of an example application that makes use of a custom notification to configure and present dynamic content to the user within a notification alert.

35. A WatchKit Inline Notification Text Reply Tutorial

As outlined in the chapter entitled *An Overview of Notifications in WatchKit*, notifications are now able to accept text input from the user and pass that input along to the corresponding WatchKit app. In this chapter, the example created in *A WatchKit Custom Notification Tutorial* will be extended to include the option for the user to input text via the custom notification panel.

35.1 Adding the Inline Reply Action

Begin by launching Xcode and opening the *CustomNotifyApp* project. Once loaded, locate and edit the *AppDelegate.swift* file and modify the *didFinishLaunchingWithOptions* method so that it reads as follows:

```
func application(application: UIApplication, didFinishLaunchingWithOptions
launchOptions: [NSObject: AnyObject]?) -> Bool {

    let replyAction: UIMutableUserNotificationAction =
        UIMutableUserNotificationAction()
    replyAction.identifier = "REPLY_IDENTIFIER"
    replyAction.title = "Reply"
    replyAction.destructive = false
    replyAction.authenticationRequired = false
    replyAction.behavior = .TextInput

    let notificationCategory:UIMutableUserNotificationCategory =
        UIMutableUserNotificationCategory()

    notificationCategory.identifier = "WEATHER_CATEGORY"

    notificationCategory.setActions([replyAction],
        forContext: UIUserNotificationActionContext.Default)

    let settings = UIUserNotificationSettings(forTypes:
        [UIUserNotificationType.Sound,
```

```
        UIUserNotificationType.Alert,
        UIUserNotificationType.Badge],
        categories: [notificationCategory])

    application.registerUserNotificationSettings(settings)

    return true
}
```

The code in this method now creates a user notification action configured to display "Reply" with the behavior set to request text input and then uses this configuration when registering the notification.

Compile and run the CustomNotifyApp WatchKit App and, once the updated WatchKit app has installed on the Apple Watch or Simulator, launch the companion iOS app and tap on either the Snow or Rain button. Immediately lock the screen on the iPhone and make sure that the Apple Watch screen is active. After the delay has elapsed the notification should appear on the display as shown in Figure 35-1. Note that in addition to the Dismiss button, the Reply action button now also appears within the notification:

Figure 35-1

35.2 Configuring Text Input Suggestions

In order to obtain a list of input suggestions, a call will be made by the WatchKit framework to the *suggestionsForResponseToActionWithIdentifier* method of the notification controller class. This method is passed the notification category identifier and the notification object and expects in return an array of String objects containing the suggested text to be displayed in the text input screen. Locate the *NotificationController.swift* file in the Project Navigator panel and add the *suggestionsForResponseToActionWithIdentifier* method so that it reads as follows:

```
override func suggestionsForResponseToActionWithIdentifier(identifier:
String, forLocalNotification localNotification: UILocalNotification,
inputLanguage: String) -> [String] {

    let suggestions = ["Bring an Umbrella", "Pack Snow Gear"]
    return suggestions
}
```

Repeat the previous steps to install the WatchKit app and trigger the notification from the iOS app. When the notification appears on the Apple Watch or Simulator, tap the Reply button and note that the suggested input options are listed and available for selection:

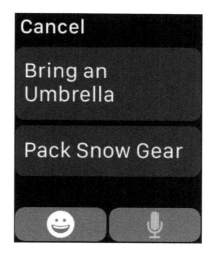

Figure 35-2

35.3 Handling the Text Input Action

The final task in implementing text input with a notification is to handle the input once it has been submitted by the user. When text has been input for a local notification, the *handleActionWithIdentifier:forLocalNotification:withResponseInfo:* method of the extension delegate will be called and passed the notification category identifier, the notification object and the user response info dictionary. Contained within the dictionary is a key-value pair where the key is set to *UIUserNotificationActionResponseTypedTextKey* and the value is the text that was provided by the user. Select the *ExtensionDelegate.swift* file and implement this method now so that it reads as follows:

```
func handleActionWithIdentifier(identifier: String?, forLocalNotification
localNotification: UILocalNotification, withResponseInfo responseInfo:
[NSObject : AnyObject]) {

        print(responseInfo[UIUserNotificationActionResponseTypedTextKey])
```

```
}
```

For the purposes of testing, this method simply prints the entered text to the Xcode console.

35.4 Testing the App

Compile and run the app once again and trigger the notification so that it is displayed on the Apple Watch or Watch Simulator. Tap the Reply button and use either the dictation or suggested input values to input text.

35.5 Summary

This chapter has added support for notification inline text replies to the custom notification app created in the preceding chapter. This involved the addition of a user notification action configured for text input, the declaration of suggested input strings and the implementation of a handler within the Watch app extension delegate class.

Index

Index

www.ingramcontent.com/pod-product-compliance
Lightning Source LLC
Chambersburg PA
CBHW062110050326
40690CB00016B/3272

9 781517 365059